MW01609930

365 DAYS IN *Proverbs*

WISDOM FOR LIFE

BroadStreet
PUBLISHING

BroadStreet Publishing Group, LLC.
Savage, Minnesota, USA
Broadstreetpublishing.com

9781424566365

Devotional entries composed by Brenna Stockman.

Typesetting and design by Garborg Design Works | garborgdesign.com
Editorial services by Michelle Winger | literallyprecise.com and Sarah Eral.

Printed in China.

23 24 25 26 27 28 29 7 6 5 4 3 2 1

Wisdom is far more valuable than rubies.
Nothing you desire can compare with it.

Proverbs 8:11 NLT

Intro

Wise sayings and good advice can touch the present, but how much better is wisdom that strengthens the eternal soul? As the king of Israel, Solomon had access to riches most of us could only dream of, yet he spoke of wisdom as the most prized treasure. It is described as more precious than gold and rubies.

The book of Proverbs is full of practical advice with physical and spiritual benefits. As you meditate on these proverbs, devotional entries, and prayers, lean into the knowledge revealed in God's living Word. Jesus is wisdom personified; he is always ready with revelation to expand our understanding. The fountain of his life pours into our hearts every time we search after him. His wisdom is full of loving leadership, calm confidence, and honest conviction. There truly is no better thing to pursue in this life.

Find treasures of wisdom as you turn your attention to Jesus and listen for his voice in the stillness. You can build a hopeful future on the foundation of his love with wisdom as your guide.

January
The fear of the LORD
is the beginning of knowledge;
fools despise wisdom and discipline.
PROVERBS 1:7 CSB

Solomon the Wise

These are the proverbs of Solomon, David's son, king of Israel.
PROVERBS 1:1 NLT

As we begin our journey through Proverbs, let's consider the position of Solomon, the author of most of the book. Solomon was the son of David and Bathsheba and the third king of the united kingdoms of Israel and Judah after Saul and David. He ruled for forty years in the late 900s BC and was recognized for his wisdom which God gifted when Solomon prayed for guidance as a new and insecure ruler. Solomon's wisdom was known throughout the world, and he was "richer and wiser than any other king on earth" (1 Kings 10:23).

Since God did not allow David to build the temple because he was a warrior (1 Chronicles 28:3), David prepared the workers and materials for his son to be the builder. Solomon built other projects as well, but the temple was the opus project of his life.

Lord, please focus my attention on Proverbs and your words through Solomon, so I may gain wisdom to live my best life.

Wise Words

They teach wisdom and self-control;
they will help you understand wise words.
PROVERBS 1:2 NCV

There is little point in reading anything without understanding it. God's Word is a seed that is planted in our hearts to nurture us into mature believers. This can't happen without repentance and fertile ground in our hearts and minds. Solomon addresses the need for understanding right from the beginning of Proverbs so we can see the noteworthy characteristics of wisdom at once.

A heart open to the Word of God is teachable, and this will lead to wisdom and self-control. Comprehension comes from the Holy Spirit moving in us as we read and learn under the teaching of wise King Solomon.

Dear Father, give me a fertile heart and a teachable mind to learn from Proverbs. May I understand the difference between wisdom and folly.

Purpose of Proverbs

Their purpose is to teach people
to live disciplined and successful lives,
to help them do what is right, just, and fair.
PROVERBS 1:3 NLT

The world bombards us with subjective truth and redefined words. Today's verse is clear that if you want insight and understanding, the Word of God is there for you. You will not be led astray if you stay close to God in prayer and attentively read your Bible. Proverbs in particular addresses what wisdom looks like in practical life.

We struggle with selfishness as humans. We want to indulge ourselves in comfort and excess. This sidetracks us from the life God intends for us. Learning to be wise will lead us to lives both disciplined and successful. If we lean into the discipline from God, we will learn to do what is right, fair, and just and reach true success.

Dear Lord, open my eyes to see the folly in my life so I can address it. Let me not just accept your discipline but appreciate it for the blessing it is.

Impact of Proverbs

To give prudence to the simple,
To the young man knowledge and discretion.
PROVERBS 1:4 NKJV

Prudence is when a person shows wisdom and shrewdness in managing their affairs. They have skill and good judgment when using personal resources. They show caution and circumspection in the face of danger or risk, and they can discipline themselves because they possess reasoning.

In our verse today, God says this heightened level of behavior is given even to the simplest and youngest of people. God does not make unreasonable demands on us, and he promises to gift us with behaviors and characteristics to carry us through life.

Father, give me a repentant heart and a contrite spirit to hear your voice. I want to follow your teaching even when others say I am wrong.

Lifelong Learning

Wise people can also listen and learn;
even they can find good advice in these words.
PROVERBS 1:5 NCV

We seek wisdom not for our glory but so we are better prepared to help others. The purpose of God's wisdom is communal and not individual. The Bible is full of wisdom both accessible and understandable to everyone. If we think we are already wise, we can still glean more wisdom from the pages of Scripture.

Let's strive to always grow in wisdom and understanding because we are never too wise to learn more about God and his majesty. In the Bible, how often do we see examples of God using seemingly simple people, like children or fishermen, to be recipients of his wisdom and change the world? Pride blocks the flow of wisdom, but a humble heart will receive it. Humility is required to grow in wisdom.

Dear God, please continue to grow me in wisdom and teach me from your Word. Open my ears to hear and my heart to understand.

Wise Riddles

Anyone can understand wise words and stories,
the words of the wise and their riddles.
PROVERBS 1:6 NCV

Solomon wrote these words to his children to assure them that no kingship, scholarly education, a good upbringing is needed to understand the Word of the Lord. The Lord does not speak in riddles to confuse us but to separate those who desire to learn from those who aren't willing to put in the effort to understand. No matter our situation, we have access to God's wisdom and the ability to become wise.

Like Solomon, when we receive wisdom, we ought to pass it along. He wanted his children to grow in love and understanding of God, so he encouraged them to receive his wisdom and learn from his life. Let's openly share ourselves the same way and pass our wisdom on to others.

Father, teach me to become wise and give me opportunities to share my wisdom with others. Thank you for explaining your riddles to me when I choose to humbly listen.

Fear of the Lord

The fear of the LORD is the beginning of knowledge,
But fools despise wisdom and instruction.
PROVERBS 1:7 NKJV

What does it mean to fear the Lord? Our loving Father doesn't want us hiding from him, guilt-ridden and ashamed, like Adam and Eve in the Garden of Eden. He wants us to have a healthy reverence that leads to lives of obedience and worship. He is King of the universe and fully worthy of our respect and honor.

Sin should scare us because it's direct disobedience against the Creator who loves and sustains our souls, and sin carries consequences. Fearing the Lord is an appropriate response to understanding his position and greatness. Disrespecting God by insisting on our ways is neither wise nor beneficial. He knows and wants what is best for us, and he is best for us.

Lord, I want to worship you with my life instead of wasting years chasing my desires. You are my King, and the healthy fear I have for you reminds me that the best choices I can make are aligned with your will.

Loving Discipline

Listen, my son, to your father's instruction
and do not forsake your mother's teaching.
They are a garland to grace your head
and a chain to adorn your neck.
PROVERBS 1:8-9 NIV

Discipline can seem distasteful, and we try to avoid it, but loving parents discipline their children. God, our loving Father, wants what is best for us. When we heed his discipline, it's as if we clothe ourselves in fine garlands and jewelry; the change in our lives will be apparent.

Whether or not we had good parents who raised us to be disciplined adults, we have a heavenly Father guiding us down the best path. Let's not despise his hand of correction, for it teaches us to walk in wisdom and keeps us from falling into pits of sin. Some lessons are difficult to learn, and sometimes discipline is harsh, but if we remain teachable, we will reap his blessings.

Lord, please teach and guide me. I will not despise your discipline but embrace it because it comes from your great love. I never want to forget the lessons you have taught me.

When Sinners Lead

My child, if sinners try to lead you into sin,
do not follow them.
PROVERBS 1:10 NCV

Following God means we forfeit following others. Sometimes God places people and angels in our lives to lead us in his purposes, and with time spent with him, we can discern those people from sinners trying to entice us in directions that conflict with God's plan. A person who does not spend time with God will not know his voice from the other voices crowding daily life. We will miss or even choose to ignore the wisdom that would take us to where God wants us to be.

Our Father addresses us as children for a good reason. We have childish tendencies if we do not mature in the Word which leads to life and goodness. Without this maturity, we tend to allow the sinners in our lives to convince us to sin. Following them down wrong paths will require repentance and repair before we are back in the light of God's plan.

Dear Lord, make and mold me in your image. Lead me closer to you rather than allowing me to be distracted by sinners leading me into sin.

Wisdom Isn't Silent

Wisdom calls aloud outside;
She raises her voice in the open squares.
PROVERBS 1:20 NKJV

Job 28:28 tells us, "The fear of the Lord, that is wisdom, and to depart from evil is understanding." Wisdom is not a quiet, personal virtue; it is obvious and has a great impact on those around us. Wisdom is active: it calls aloud and departs from evil. Wisdom leaves a trail and a legacy.

What is our legacy? How is wisdom evident in our lives? Does the way we act under pressure or hardship reveal the trust we have in our Maker? Do we stay out of drama and gossip? Are we planning and making smart decisions for our future? Wisdom calls aloud; she doesn't stay silent. What is our impact? Whom are we influencing? How are we known? Is the influence of God on us evident to everyone watching how we live?

Father God, please show me how to walk wisely. Teach me when to speak and when to stay silent, when to step forward and when to wait. Help me depart from any evil that tries to ensnare me.

Wisdom Calls

She calls to the crowds along the main street,
to those gathered in front of the city gate.
PROVERBS 1:21 NLT

In biblical times, city gates were a place of business. Transactions were made, connections formed, and decisions solidified that affected the community. Provision and protection formed in this important location, and people gathered so they would know what was happening with those around them. When Solomon said wisdom calls to the crowds on the main street and the city gate, he was impressing upon us the importance of spreading wisdom to as many people as possible and especially to those making decisions for everyone. Let everyone hear the good news of how to take the wise path.

We would be wise to not just learn wisdom but to speak about it as well. Let it be a topic of conversation so we can encourage others to make good decisions and live well. The more we think about wisdom, the less we will be distracted by folly.

My Father, make me bold about your heart and discipline. Allow me enough humility to show others that any wisdom in me comes from you.

Repent When Rebuked

"Repent at my rebuke!
Then I will pour out my thoughts to you,
I will make known to you my teachings."
PROVERBS 1:23 NIV

As we learn about wisdom, we naturally take our old behaviors into account, and that is good. Learning from our failures is a solid way to identify Christ-like traits, but God's thoughts don't stop there. His teachings move us forward instead of freezing us in the moment.

Repentance is a necessary step toward a wise character. It is a key element resulting from humble acceptance of the truth of our sinful nature. Sin is infused into every cell of our hearts, minds, and bodies, but it is all washed as clean as snow when we repent. We are a new creation free to accept God's thoughts and teachings.

Dear Lord, you are my all-in-all. You are my purpose and path. You define my existence and my eternity. May my life reflect your wisdom.

Impact of Unrepentance

"Then you will call to me, but I will not answer.
You will look for me, but you will not find me.
It is because you rejected knowledge
and did not choose to respect the Lord."
Proverbs 1:28-29 NCV

There are three things happening in today's excerpt from Proverbs. Some people ignore God's call, some look for God but don't find him, and some reject the truth and thus disrespect God. If God calls and we ignore that voice, we potentially lose the opportunity to have his help when we need it most. Our choices made in good times will reflect in God's response when we need him in challenging times. There are consequences to our choices, and it is prudent to have God foremost in our hearts.

It is dangerous to listen to the temptations of Satan, but it is equally dangerous to ignore the voice of God. Once we have walked away from him, the divergence from his path becomes increasingly obvious in our lives. The warning in these words is clear and concise: one poor choice can lead to dire consequences.

Lord my God, let me hear your voice as I seek your wisdom. Don't allow me to be waylaid or sidelined by any distraction.

Bitter Fruit

"They rejected my advice
and paid no attention when I corrected them.
Therefore, they must eat the bitter fruit of living their own way,
choking on their own schemes."
PROVERBS 1:30-31 NLT

According to Mark 3:22-30, the only unforgivable sin is the blasphemy of the Holy Spirit. "All sin and blasphemy can be forgiven, but anyone who blasphemes the Holy Spirit will never be forgiven" (vv. 28-29). So what does our verse today mean?

It's about consequences. When we make plans and pay no attention to God, we are laying a path away from holiness and the path God intended for us. The consequences of that decision are bitter fruit. Ultimately, the bitter fruit causes us to choke. We can't sin freely and toss in a prayer of repentance at the end of the day. Our minds and hearts will solidify into a self-track rather than a God-track. We can turn that train around through prayer and reading the Word, but it takes diligence and the moving of the Holy Spirit in our hearts.

Lord Almighty, you are my advisor and authority. You are my heart and mind. Guide me and make me more like you.

Complacency Kills

"The simple are killed by their turning away, and the complacency of fools destroys them."
PROVERBS 1:32 ESV

Doing nothing is a choice. Being lackadaisical will eventually destroy a person. Turning away from God will kill the soul. Make no mistake, dear believer; you are choosing something when you choose nothing. God tells us throughout Proverbs and the whole Bible that we are to seek him and serve him and his sheep. We are to spread his beautiful, life-restoring message and live redeemed and humble lives. Each of these commands are actions. They require a purposeful heart and mind which is the opposite of complacency.

Throughout the Word, God also promises to equip us for the work he has set out for us. "May the God of peace… equip you with everything good that you may do his will, working in us that which is pleasing in his sight" (Hebrews 13:20-21). You are wise to avoid complacency in your life and lean on God's help.

Dear God, may I always attend to you and whatever you have planned for me. Help me rest when I need rest and act when I should act.

Live without Fear

"Those who listen to me will live in safety and be at peace, without fear of injury."
PROVERBS 1:33 NCV

Listening to God's wisdom changes everything about us. We don't have the same perspective on this earthly life with God's wisdom directing our paths. While the world swirls around us in conflict and upheaval, we are covered by his protection and provision. Eternity is real, and it's really waiting for us.

When we are focused on the things of God, the things of the world fade. We may be rich or poor, sick or healthy, old or young, but when we are overcome by God's love for us and ours for him, we have eternal eyes that see what lays ahead. We are going to a place without pain, fear, grief, or loss. We can live in a way that reflects the truth of our eternity.

Lord, I am in an earthly life, but I want to reflect an eternal life. May my presence be a soothing balm to those needing to hear about the God who gives me safety and peace.

Focus and Listen

My child, listen to what I say and remember what I command you. Listen carefully to wisdom; set your mind on understanding.
PROVERBS 2:1-2 NCV

Hearing means being aware of by ear or perceiving. To *listen* means to hear with thoughtful consideration. Today's verse reveals the difference between these two words by instructing us to set our minds on understanding. Hearing the words of the Bible is not the same as fully understanding the meaning and intention behind the words. Seeking wisdom requires us to pray and request understanding, and understanding is the difference between wisdom and no wisdom.

The writer of this proverb starts by drawing our attention with "my child." Most of us have attempted to gain the focus of a child to instruct them. We insist on focused attention, speak clearly, and follow through with consequences. Parenting and teaching children requires all three of these steps, and the Lord has promised he will do nothing less for us.

Dear Father, please be patient with me as I seek understanding by being focused on your Word, teachable in my mind and heart, and alert to the consequences of my decisions.

Seeking Silver

Cry out for insight, and ask for understanding.
Search for them as you would for silver;
seek them like hidden treasures.

PROVERBS 2:3-4 NLT

Silver is typically not found in handy little nuggets. It is mixed in long veins with a variety of ores and metals. In biblical times, silver mining was dangerous and was often performed by slaves, many of whom lost their lives doing this dangerous work. After the veins of mixed metals and ores were removed from the earth, they had to be refined. Isaiah 48:10 speaks about silver being refined in a furnace, as does Proverbs 27:21. Ezekiel 22:18 mentions using bellows to extract silver from the ores. Exodus 31:3-5 outlines the specialized level of skills necessary for working with silver and other metals.

It is our honor and responsibility as believers to seek after wisdom in the Word of God with this level of diligence and attention. The Word is easily understood by a child, but wisdom is gained by truly focusing on searching, or mining, the Scriptures with increasing skill and attention throughout our lives.

Dear God, I seek the Word with all the baggage of my daily life, yet I desire your wisdom.

Human Understanding

The Lord grants wisdom!
From his mouth come knowledge and understanding.
Proverbs 2:6 NLT

What is the difference between human understanding and God's wisdom? Solomon was the wisest man to ever live, and he attributed all his wisdom to God. He knew he was only wise by God's grace.

The world's knowledge can't give us what we're truly looking for. Empty insight is the best the world has to offer, but God's Word is filled with hope and answers for the wise. We may become humanly wise through our ambitions, but true wisdom comes only from God. If we want to become wise, it starts with seeking the Lord. The more we listen to him, spend time with him, and obey his Word, the wiser we become as our hearts and minds align with his.

Oh God, you give us wisdom when we ask, and you fill us with understanding when we seek you. No amount of knowledge found in this world can compare to the sweetness of knowing and understanding you.

Our Shield

He stores up sound wisdom for the upright;
He is a shield to those who walk in integrity.
Proverbs 2:7 nasb

Life can feel overwhelming at times, but how comforting is it to know God never leaves us alone? He is our shield against evil and our strength when we have nothing left. When we need wisdom, he pours his out for us and leads us down the right path.

We can confidently walk through the darkness of this world with integrity and wisdom because we know he is protecting us on all sides from any plots and devices our enemy brings against us. He has already accounted for anything that concerns us and made the proper provisions. Let's live uprightly, without worry or compromise, knowing our heavenly Father has everything under control.

Lord, thank you for watching over me. No matter what comes against me, I know I will prevail because you fight my battles. I will walk forward with surety and integrity, for you are my shield and confidence. You are always with me; you will never leave me on my own.

He Guards Us

He guards the paths of the just
and protects those who are faithful to him.
PROVERBS 2:8 NLT

When life gives us lemons, we might decide God has forsaken us or we have done something wrong. There's no sign of him guarding our paths or protecting us at all. If our days are filled with tragedy and burdens, this is the logical conclusion, right? Not so.

God assures us he has protected our eternal lives, but this earthly life is riddled with trials and tribulations. Tough times are not a reflection of God's negligence but rather of his purpose being fulfilled. He desires us to mature to be more like Jesus. He wants our lives to reflect him, so others are drawn to the kingdom. Our faith in him will shine into the lives of those around us. Do not be misled by sin (Proverbs 13:6) but have faith in the one who guards your soul. He will repay each person for their actions.

Dear Jesus, please open my eyes to your hand in my life. Show me where you have guarded and protected me. Show me the steps I need to take to stay on the path you have set for me.

The Good Path

Then you will discern righteousness, justice,
And integrity, and every good path.
PROVERBS 2:9 NASB

True wisdom is acquired by staying close to God in the Word and by seeking understanding by knowing him. This doesn't happen overnight, and it can't happen without effort. It also doesn't mean more work equals a relationship with God. Instead, as your heart turns toward God by reading his Word and seeking him, the blessings of that relationship will start to show.

The blessing of being close to your Maker is true discernment. You will be able to see the difference between justice and injustice. You will know when a person behaves with integrity, and you will appreciate it. You will be able to make decisions that lead to good paths. The blessing of your effort to know and stay close to God will be a life filled with truth and wisdom. This is no easy task, but it is a worthy one.

Father, please open my eyes. Please give me the desire to seek you in the Word and make you my priority. May I see through your eyes and to hear with your ears so I can discern the righteous path.

Delight in Wisdom

Wisdom will enter your heart,
And knowledge will be delightful to your soul.
PROVERBS 2:10 NASB

Sin makes people blind. When we see this blindness in others, we are acutely aware that without God, we would be just as blind or even more so. The deeper we go in our relationship with God, the further we sink into humility and the awareness of our inability to gain wisdom without the guiding hand of our loving Lord. May we always be dependent on him.

This humility and awareness of our deficiencies does not lead to a lack of confidence. We rejoice in our dependence on God because true knowledge comes only from him. There is energy and beauty in this assurance. What a relief to know we do not carry that burden. God alone is the delight of our souls. He alone gives wisdom.

Jesus, I rely on you so much. Please keep my eyes on you and give me the yearning for your presence that leads to a fulfilling and pleasing life. May my life edify and bless you.

Guides and Protects

Good sense will protect you;
understanding will guard you.
PROVERBS 2:11 NCV

It makes sense that "good sense" leads to better decisions than bad sense, but is it true that understanding is a guard of some sort? Yes. In other versions of the Bible, good sense is translated as discretion or wise choices. Discretion is the ability to judge or make responsible decisions. You can't really have good sense or discretion without understanding. God has already assured us that we gain understanding when we seek wisdom in his Word.

Our eyes can't be open to the truth of any situation without the Holy Spirit. John 14:26 tells us the Holy Spirit is our teacher. He convicts us of our sin, and he is our source of revelation, wisdom, and power. We can't understand without the Holy Spirit who is in us. Leaning on God through his Holy Spirit gives the believer insight that guides, guards, and protects.

Holy Spirit, please fill my soul with the truth and give me understanding. Please allow understanding to flourish in me so I gain good sense.

Perverse Speech

It will rescue you from the way of evil,
from anyone who says perverse things.
PROVERBS 2:12 CSB

There are protections and provisions built into wisdom. We can't gain wisdom without the guidance and teaching of the Holy Spirit who dwells within us. We don't have good sense or discernment without wisdom, but once we have it, the way of evil is closed to believers who have gained wisdom by reading the Word and focusing on it.

There are two paths in life: one that leads to God and one that leads away from him. It is reassuring to know the way of evil is not an option if we stay close to God and rely on his wisdom. As part of this protection, believers are saved from people who speak perversely. Other translations of the Bible use the words *twisted*, *contradictions*, or *liars*. Wisdom protects us from them, and that is comforting.

Father, speak your wisdom into my heart and allow me to see the way of truth and avoid the way of evil. Give me eyes to see and ears to hear when people speak perversely so I may recognize their lies and contradictions.

Two Paths

Follow the steps of the good,
and stay on the paths of the righteous.
PROVERBS 2:20 NLT

Staying on the paths of the righteous is pivotal because, as the verse prior to this one warns, sin leads to death. Our loving and gracious God is willing and able to save us from our self-inflicted demise, but it requires us to stop walking in the way of sin and start walking in the way of the righteous.

There are always consequences for our choices: good or bad. Whether we follow God or follow our sinful desires, the destination is explained to us in Proverbs. The choice is ours. We can't expect to partake in God's inheritance if we have not lived like his children, but God has promised wonderful things to those who follow him and live righteously.

When faced with two paths—two choices—I will choose you, dear God. More than anything else, I want you. Sometimes my judgment is clouded by my earthly desires. When that happens, please break through the fog and remind me which path leads back to you. Teach me to follow your steps and walk like you.

Where You Will Live

The upright will live in the land,
and the blameless will remain in it.
PROVERBS 2:21 NIV

A blessing of wisdom is having a place to live. Solomon says in Psalm 37:9, "Those who are evil will be destroyed, but those who hope in the Lord shall inherit the land." However, blessings aren't always evident in this lifetime. The Lord states throughout Proverbs 2 that there are consequences for seeking him and his wisdom and equally dire results for those who choose not to seek wisdom. The choice may be here and now, but for eternity, we will remain in the presence of God.

As Christians, we do not have to concern ourselves with where we will reside. Faith in God is our all-in-all story because we trust him to work out the details. That doesn't mean there won't be difficulties or stress in the moment, but the story is already written, and our eternal home is already determined. We have the land, and we will remain in it.

Dear Father, please increase my faith so I can see you here. Please heal my heart so I know you have already determined where I will be. Give me wisdom to know you are the beginning and the end.

God Removes the Wicked

The wicked will be removed from the land,
and the treacherous will be uprooted.
PROVERBS 2:22 NLT

Not only will believers be living in God's land, but the evildoers will not be there. People who have sadly chosen to defy the Lord and reject his wisdom will be uprooted and denied eternity with the Creator. The blessings of following God are not always evident in this lifetime, but the consequences of rejecting his wisdom will be played out for eternity for those who reject him. May this truth motivate us to reach out to our unbelieving friends and family.

Dear Christian, live your life as a testimony to God who is the author of wisdom. May you see the fruit of a life well lived as other people desire what you have. May the people around you pay attention to your discretion, humility, and discernment. May you have the words needed to reach these loved ones for God.

Lord Jesus, may I resound with your Spirit as I live my daily life. May my loved ones seek what I have and resolve to learn about this wisdom which only comes from you.

Length of Days

Do not forget my law,
But let your heart keep my commands;
For length of days and long life
And peace they will add to you.
Proverbs 3:1-2 NKJV

God created his world and everything in it with wisdom and grace. He orchestrated the laws of gravity and thermodynamics to ensure everything works together for good. Even our fallen planet is structured so his goodness will prevail over evil. Momentary evil will be overcome by glory.

Within the lives of God's people, God's goodness also has overriding strength. When we live within the laws the Lord has specifically structured and orchestrated for our blessing, we will see those blessings play out in a longer life and peaceful existence. He has said it; it is so.

Father, I love your laws and your creation. I love to follow you all my days which you have told me will be many when I live your ways. Thank you for your many blessings.

Loyal and Kind

Never let loyalty and kindness leave you!
Tie them around your neck as a reminder.
Write them deep within your heart.
PROVERBS 3:3 NLT

Loyalty and kindness are so valuable, God tells us to tie them around our necks and write them on our hearts. A betraying, cruel person is detestable; a loyal, kind person is highly desirable. These virtues are sought after in spouses, employees, team members, leaders, and almost any other position. We want to lead, follow, and be around loyal, kind people. Jesus offered us the ultimate example of loyalty and kindness when he shared his life with us: from his birth to his death and continuing eternally afterwards.

In a world of self-seeking hearts, God knew loyalty and kindness would not be easy mandates to maintain, so he showed us how to walk them out with his own life, and he instructed us with strong metaphors like tying them to our necks and writing them on our hearts.

Oh Lord, the kindness and loyalty you have shown me is unmatched. I want to be kind and loyal as well; hide these virtues deep in my heart so I can be like you.

Esteemed

Find favor and high esteem
In the sight of God and man.
PROVERBS 3:4 NKJV

A person who is highly esteemed has gone beyond expectations. They have invested in relationships, maintained a disciplined life, and built a respectable reputation. This person is noble in the eyes of the public as well as in private where only God bears witness. This type of person works through conflict, embraces challenge, does what is right even when nobody seems to notice, and isn't swayed by the majority opinion. They know the best things in life are worth fighting for and don't come easily or quickly. They are kind, patient, and loving.

This esteemed person finds favor with God and with others, not because they are lucky, but because they have a legacy of being reliable and good. A person like this is not perfect, but they are aware of their weaknesses and go to God for help. They use their strengths to serve the Lord and others, and they are trusted with more responsibility because of their faithfulness. Let's strive for this in the sight of God first and others as well.

By your strength and for your glory, I strive to live nobly, dear God.

February
Guard your heart above all else,
for it is the source of life.
Proverbs 4:23

Leaning on the Lord

Trust in the Lord with all your heart,
And lean not on your own understanding.
PROVERBS 3:5 NKJV

We look to God for direction and understanding because this world is notorious for mixed signals and unclear instructions. Our perspective is linear and limited, but God's point of view is perfect and endless. How can we fully trust ourselves when we are temporal and flawed? It is safe and best to put our trust in him.

Even in our carefully crafted plans, let's stay adaptable when God decides to intervene. We will always receive the greatest outcome when we remain positioned to receive God's direction instead of clinging to our agendas. When the path becomes murky, God guides us through. Song of Solomon 8:5 offers us a picture of God's beloved coming out of the desert while leaning on him. Let's lean on God today and trust he will guide us through.

I am ready to trust you completely with my life, Father God. Help me lean on your grace instead of my understanding. You are always faithful, and no matter what I'm dealing with, I know you will bring me through it.

Acknowledge God

In all your ways acknowledge Him,
And He will make your paths straight.
PROVERBS 3:6 NASB

King Solomon was no stranger to self-pursuit, and he wanted better for his son. He had learned his lesson; self-indulgence leads to crooked, confusing paths. All the worldly wealth imaginable was at his fingertips, but he chose to acknowledge the Lord in everything. Everything he was, had, or did was by the Lord's doing, and Solomon knew that. He walked a clear, straight path when he fixed his eyes on God.

Whenever he took his eyes off God and became distracted by some worldly pursuit, his life would begin to unravel. Being the wisest man who ever lived, Solomon acknowledged God and chose to walk his path as best he could. We avoid a lot of unnecessary trouble when we choose to acknowledge God in all things and walk in his way.

I want to walk in your ways, oh God. Even when your path seems more difficult, I know your strength will lead me through. I acknowledge you in everything and recognize your way is best.

Strong Bones

It will be health to your flesh,
And strength to your bones.
PROVERBS 3:8 NKJV

Before this verse, Solomon talks about God's understanding versus human understanding. At no point do humans have a better point of view than God has, and we can lean into that knowledge. We can embrace the fact that our Creator, who made us and adores us, knows what is best for us. A healthy dependency on our God is the quickest way to find the most gracious way to live.

According to verse six, the first step to a good life is to acknowledge God in everything we do. Check in with the Almighty with your plans and wait for his go-ahead before solidifying the next step. He assures us his way leads to health in our flesh and strength in our bones.

Dear Lord, I pray for mercy and truth around my neck. I love your ways, and I need to be close to you. Forgive me my sins which start small but take me off your chosen way.

First Comes God

Honor the L*ORD* *with your possessions,*
And with the firstfruits of all your increase.
Proverbs 3:9 NKJV

Minimalism is becoming more popular in western culture, but the Lord isn't necessarily asking us to give up everything. He does ask that we give to him first. If we only acquire what he gives us as blessings, maintaining what we own will be less of a burden and more of an honor. Ownership is a responsibility, and when we put time and effort into our possessions, we are not using that time and effort in our relationships.

If you review every bottle of specialty sauce in your fridge, every purse in your closet, and every device you own as either a blessing or a burden, suddenly possessions become things that either forward the kingdom or don't. If we have comfortable furniture for people to sit on when they come for Bible study or a good visit, it's a blessing. If we have a home that is never shared or used to serve somehow, that's indulgence. Everything we own is to be a blessing to forward the kingdom or as a special gift for us from God. That's the goal.

Lord, show me my possessions through your eyes. Nurture in me a heart fully given to you so I can own without burden or guilt.

Full Barns

Your barns will be filled with plenty,
And your vats will overflow with new wine.
PROVERBS 3:10 NKJV

The consequence of sin is death (Romans 6:23), but repentance leads to everlasting life (Luke 13:5). In other words, there is sin in all of us. Repentance is a choice. Following God's path is how blessings, especially eternal ones, start to flow, but Scripture is clear that there are also blessings before eternity.

In our verse today, God says we will see abundance when we behave with wisdom. This starts with giving first to God when we are blessed. When we gain from our work and efforts, the first thing we need to do is to give back to God. We can do this by blessing a family in need or giving to the church so they can bless people. We can give generously with our time; we can spend time with God interceding for people who need prayers. We can ask God how he wants us to show gratefulness.

Lord, may my heart be contrite and open to you. Show me when you want me to be active and when you want me to be still. May I always acknowledge you in both my blessings and trials which bring me closer to you.

Don't Despise Correction

Do not despise the chastening of the LORD,
Nor detest His correction.
PROVERBS 3:11 NKJV

Tough times. Sometimes it feels like all the blessings went somewhere else. Sometimes hard work doesn't pay off. Sometimes we eat all the good stuff and do all the right workouts, but our bodies are still sick or weak. What is going on?

The book of Job is a good read for understanding things when nothing makes sense. The background message in Job is to trust the Lord through every hardship because it isn't always about us. God gives us blessings and allows some challenges as well, but the purpose of either one is still left to him. We need levels of discipline at different times, and we go through seasons of testing. The goal is to receive both blessings and trials with an eye to learning more about our Savior and honoring him through the season we're in.

I lift my eyes toward you, Lord. Whether this season is easier or more difficult, let me see where I can grow.

Correcting His Beloved

Whom the LORD loves He corrects,
Just as a father the son in whom he delights.
PROVERBS 3:12 NKJV

Although there will be times of blessing, the Christian life is not one of ease. When our hearts and minds wander down a spiritually unproductive path, our loving Father will bring us back, and that often means discipline.

Many difficult challenges effectively work to bring the Father's children back to himself. We can experience loss, poverty, sickness or other physical challenges, and alienation. The list goes on. Sometimes we experience discipline from another person, like an elder or pastor, when they speak truth into our situation. A friend can lead with truth and love if we're messing up, or we can be led by the Holy Spirit to change our attitude or behavior.

Lord, whenever you press upon me to change, please open my heart to it and show me the path through it.

Finding Wisdom

Blessed is the person who finds wisdom.
And one who obtains understanding.
PROVERBS 3:13 NASB

How blessed we are to receive God's gifts and be led by his hand. We must never quit our search for his wisdom because wisdom from God is far superior to anything this world offers. Daily, let's read God's Word and spend time listening to him. That is how we become more like him; that is how we gain understanding. We learn the heart and mind of God by growing in relationship with him.

His path is wisdom and truth. He wants to share his wisdom and understanding with us. We must strive to stay humble, teachable, and patient while we attune to God's voice. Let's learn from him and enjoy an incredible relationship with him. He wants to share all things with us.

Father, I depend on you for wisdom and understanding. Without you, I can't find my way. I turn to your Word for guidance and familiarize myself with your ways.

Wisdom's Worth

The gain from her is better than gain from silver
and her profit better than gold.
PROVERBS 3:14 ESV

A price tag can't be placed on wisdom. A wise man is worth more than a king. So much of our lives is spent working to make a wage, but how much effort do we invest in finding wisdom? Are we truly seeking God, or just checking in from time to time? Yes, we need our daily food, but our spiritual nourishment is even more important, and we don't always realize when we're starving our souls. We could gain the whole world and lose ourselves in the process.

Commit to seeking God first. We need to desire his wisdom more than gold and more than our paychecks. We can then watch as everything either falls into place or falls away. God directs our steps and determines the course of our lives. Why not seek him instead of wasting our lives chasing what doesn't last?

God, you matter more than anything. Please help me keep a proper perspective on my daily pursuits and lifetime dreams.

Full Surrender

She is more precious than rubies,
And all the things you may desire cannot compare with her.
PROVERBS 3:15 NKJV

Matthew 13:46 tells the story of a merchant who found a pearl of great value and sold all he had to buy it. The merchant recognized that the pearl was of greater worth than everything else he owned, and so he gave everything to obtain the valuable pearl.

Similarly, everything we own in the world is not worth the price of wisdom. Our homes on earth are insignificant compared to the kingdom of God. We serve a king worth surrendering everything for. Wisdom is worth the sacrifice too. Imagine everything desirable in the entire world and lay it all at the doormat of God's kingdom. Leave it there. It's not worth your allegiance. God wants better for you and your life. What price are you willing to pay for the precious gift of wisdom?

God, I lay all my dreams, desires, and everything that's mine at your feet. Thank you for the gifts you have given me. More than anything, please give me wisdom so I may see as you do.

Both Hands

Length of days is in her right hand,
in her left hand riches and honor.
PROVERBS 3:16 NKJV

Both hands are full when we acknowledge the Lord working in our lives. Suddenly we have eyes to see and ears to hear the details of his work through us. Without knowing God, the true source, we can't see where we are being blessed. We know there are ups and downs in life, but we can't see the spiritual work in the background.

Knowing life with God is an eyes-wide-open situation means also knowing whom to credit. Giving thanks for long, wonderful days spent in service to the King is an honor. Living in his way allows us to see which riches have an eternal impact. Putting God into his proper, respected, and beloved place in our lives balances everything.

Give me awareness, Father, so I know when you have given me another wonderful blessing. I know blessings often come hidden, so please let me see what I should see.

Peaceful Paths

Her ways are ways of pleasantness,
and all her paths are peace.
PROVERBS 3:17 ESV

Wisdom is addressed as a woman who creates, just through her existence, pleasant ways, and peaceful paths. But what does it take for wisdom to exist? It takes focus; it takes diligence. It takes persistence. It's a matter of the heart.

When we turn our hearts toward Jesus, our point of view aligns with the Creator. We start to see clearly, and that allows decisions to be made in righteousness. Once we have fully entrenched ourselves in God's Word, following his path and conversing with the Lord, wisdom seeps into the tissue and sinew of our very beings. We need the Word of God to start down the pleasant way and peaceful path.

Jesus, I need you to make my way righteous. I want to start there. I know time spent with you will lead me toward wisdom, so please give me patience and persistence.

Take Hold

She is a tree of life to those who take hold of her,
And happy are all who retain her.
PROVERBS 3:18 NKJV

The tree of life has deep roots buried in fertile soil and fed by living waters. This is not a regular tree. Wisdom is not a regular characteristic. The tree of life has a strong trunk, many branches, green leaves, and healthy fruit. The same can be said about wisdom.

A strong trunk of wisdom is achieved by careful nurturing through the younger years and weathering heavy storms as maturity grows. Many branches shoot off the trunk as it can sustain the developing dependency. Green leaves grow well with plenty of sunshine and time in the light. Healthy fruit is supported on a healthy true by way of pollination and protection from damaging winds. Overall, wisdom is a tree of life.

I am in awe, Lord, of your creation. I have a growing awareness that the fullness of points toward heaven. May your people and all you have made bow down to you.

Founded by Wisdom

The Lord by wisdom founded the earth;
By understanding He established the heavens.
Proverbs 3:19 NKJV

Wisdom motivated the Lord to create the earth. It was a wise thing to make. It was what God made when he put wisdom into the moment, and that is awesome. Wisdom is then foundational to creation and we, through the redeemed relationship we enjoy with God as believers, have full access to the wisdom that founded the earth. We are his creation; we are part of that wisdom.

Where wisdom is the spiritual steam, understanding is the intellect. The heavens were established through the understanding founded in God. It is a beautiful picture we struggle to comprehend but glory in its reality. We are his workmanship. We are created to be close to him, worshiping, working, and wondering at his goodness.

Lord, make me in the way that pleases you and create in me the desire to be exactly what will bring you glory. Thank you for your earth and heavens.

Clouds Drop Dew

By His knowledge the depths were broken up,
And clouds drop down the dew.
PROVERBS 3:20 NKJV

The waters of the deep burst forth at the beginning of the flood (Genesis 7:11), and this proverb could refer to God's knowledge of the evil in the world. He then destroyed the earth and everything in it except for Noah, his family, and the chosen animals on the ark.

The earth going forward from the flood, however, was blessed with rain and dew, rivers, lakes, and oceans. Some of this was around before the flood, and some was new and different. God's knowledge provided a beautiful, habitable planet with both fresh and salt water, complete with a wonderful ecosystem that waters plants, animals, and humans from the air and the earth.

Creator God, thank you for your wonderful planet. Thank you for the rain and dew and for all the waterways that provide so much blessing.

Discretion and Wisdom

Let them not depart from your eyes,
Keep sound wisdom and discretion.
PROVERBS 3:21 NKJV

It isn't easy to have discretion since it is a condition of the heart. Discretion is the ability to show good judgment and make decisions with reservation. It allows us to pause before speaking and understand the impact of our words. It's the manifestation of wisdom taking root in the heart and spreading into behavior and speech.

We experience days when we feel far away from God and our spiritual lives are at loose ends. Negativity and bad words slip out of our mouths, and anger shows in our faces. These are red flags. Head back into the Word, repent of your sins, and pray for God to come close. He loves us and tells us freely what we need to do in those circumstances.

Alert me, God, when I'm off-kilter and need time with you. Bless me with your presence and help me understand your wisdom.

Life and Grace

They will be life to your soul
And grace to your neck.
PROVERBS 3:22 NKJV

The soul needs life. When our souls aren't fed, we get discouraged, we lose the thirst for life, and our personalities flatten. Our complexity and creativity diminish. Every person is created to be in a relationship with God, and once that's in place, everything else lines up. If deepening a relationship with God will lead us into wisdom and life for our souls, it is worth every effort.

It takes time and effort to be in any relationship and that includes one with God. Time and effort won't get you into heaven; only the resurrected and saving grace of Jesus Christ can do that. However, when you are saved, it's important to pursue that relationship and spend time growing it. Life matters, and the source of life matters the most. Beautiful grace comes with time in Christ, and it is an amazing blessing to experience.

Dear God, you are amazing. I humble myself before you; I give myself to you because you are worthy. I ask for your grace because I am helpless without it.

No Stumbling

You will walk safely in your way,
And your foot will not stumble.
PROVERBS 3:23 NKJV

Hiking is a wonderful pastime and a beautiful metaphor for walking with God. It can also be a literal walk with God if the hike is spent in prayer and conversation with God, but that's up to the hiker and the circumstances. Time walking outdoors offers fresh air for the lungs, sunlight for the face, and movement for the legs.

Walking with wisdom takes more effort than a simple walk, but it's also a worthy effort for the mind. It's smart to walk a distance that blesses and doesn't harm. It's sensible to ensure the path is not so rough that ankles will twist, or roots, rocks, or outcroppings will cause stumbling. Planning a proper time without overextending will result in feeling refreshed rather than weary.

Dear Jesus, let me know your path so I may hike toward heaven. Let me see clearly so rocks and roots don't cause me to stumble. Please pick me up when I fail and help me keep going on the worthy path.

Peaceful Sleep

When you lie down, you will not be afraid;
When you lie down, your sleep will be sweet.
Do not be afraid of sudden danger,
Nor of trouble from the wicked when it comes.
PROVERBS 3:24-25 NASB

Is your sleep peaceful? Can you go to bed with a clean conscience? Do you leave the day's worries in the hands of your capable God? It's easier to sleep at night when our trust is in God. True safety is only found in the loving arms of our Father and in the promise of his provision. Psalm 4:8 says, "In peace I will lie down and sleep, for you alone, Lord, have me dwell in safety." Acts 12:1-12 relays the story of Peter sleeping peacefully in prison even though his execution was scheduled for the morning.

Sin will keep us tossing all night. Worry and fear drive peaceful dreams away. Trusting God does not remove all trouble and trials from our lives, but it does do away with many unnecessary headaches and hardships. We're more likely to get a good night's sleep too.

Even if evil comes knocking at my door, I will not be afraid, dear God, because I have placed my life in your hands. You are my confidence in the day and my peace at night.

Confident Stepping

The LORD *will be your confidence,*
And will keep your foot from being caught.
PROVERBS 3:26 NASB

There are many snares in this life and limitless ways to get caught in sin. It feels like walking across a minefield and never knowing when something might blow up in our faces. But when we look up past the potential pitfalls and into the loving gaze of our Savior, we find the confidence to go forward.

We don't tiptoe; we run to the open arms of our Creator. He determines our steps and makes our path forward clear. We don't need to worry about getting caught or tripped up because even if we do, he will catch us. All we need to do is keep our eyes fixed on heavenly things and not become distracted by the evil in this world. Fear distracts and casts doubt over the goodness of God. He is steadfast. We can have confidence in that.

Dear God, when people conspire against me, I will come before you for the reassurance I need. When all I see around me are dangers and temptations, I will turn my face to you and remember your promises.

Generous and Timely

Do not say to your neighbor,
"Go, and come back,
And tomorrow I will give it,"
When you have it with you.
PROVERBS 3:28 NKJV

It is possible Matthew thought about this proverb a lot. He certainly knew it because he was a Jew in ancient Israel. When Matthew wrote his gospel, he wrote down Jesus' cryptic yet effective directions to the twelve apostles: "Heal the sick, cleanse the leprosy, raise the dead, cast out demons. Freely you have received, freely give" (Matthew10:8).

Solomon addressed a reluctant giver in the verse today. God Almighty doesn't appreciate it when his people have the means to bless someone and they will later, but in the moment, they choose to delay the blessing. Matthew quoted Jesus as saying "freely." This is no mistake. Give without hesitation, without reservation, and without restriction. Why? Because that is how you have been given your blessings.

Father, let me give. Open my heart to learn how to give without holding back. You gave me so much, and I want to give that way to others.

Unnecessary Strife

Do not strive with a man without cause,
If he has done you no harm.
PROVERBS 3:30 NKJV

It's important to pick your battles; it's equally important to learn not to be petty. Everyone has the capacity to get in a mood, and behavior goes downhill. Dear believer, we need to be better than that. We can give in to a bad day or negative feedback, but we need to rise above it, especially if we engage with someone who had nothing to do with what started the downhill spiral.

Go to God. We can talk to our Father at any time and in any situation. We can ask him for help with bad feelings and a lack of control. We can breathe, take a moment, and regroup with God foremost in our minds and hearts. It's best to stay the storm for a repositioning break. Let God have your worst because he can superimpose his best in your less-than-stellar moments.

Lord, my God, you are everything, and I need you. I need you to guide my tongue and keep me calm when things go badly. I don't want to be the cause of any strife. Help me be kind to all people.

Choose No Oppressor

Do not envy the oppressor,
And choose none of his ways.
PROVERBS 3:31 NKJV

People win and people lose, and bad people lose badly. Sometimes they make decisions to hurt others purposefully, and although that is unbiblical behavior, it falls within the sinful nature of man. We shouldn't be surprised when unbiblical behavior comes out of an unbiblical person.

Therein lies an opportunity. We can move in a moment when we are the victims and be amazing witnesses for the Lord. Our voices can be especially compelling when we are hurt and yet choose grace as a response. May we be strong in the face of oppression because the Lord has a message for that oppressor.

Shake my world, oh Father. Be my voice when I want to give in to worldly responses. Help me be your voice despite my weaknesses.

Grace for Humility

He scorns the scornful,
But gives grace to the humble.
PROVERBS 3:34 NKJV

The Lord knows the foundational cracks in each heart. He knows if there is an open door to his truth and his Word, and he knows if a person is turning away from him. Here's the bad news: if you scorn God, he will scorn you. This is a grievous conclusion for the Maker of everything to make about anyone. It means an eternity separated from God and glory.

There is only one alternative. We may choose to be humble. We may choose to turn our eyes toward God and follow his grace-filled directions for our lives. He knows the best ways to show us love, and he leads us on his path to everlasting life. It is beautiful and eternal.

Lord, forgive me for the times I have scorned you. Please open your arms to me, a sinner. Help me crawl back from that lowly place of not knowing you and teach me more about you. Let me know you, Father.

Don't Forget

Get wisdom and understanding.
Don't forget or ignore my words.
PROVERBS 4:5 NCV

The writer of Proverbs was Solomon the Wise. God asked him in a dream what he wanted, and Solomon asked for wisdom. God was so pleased Solomon did not ask for riches or longevity, he gave him all three: wisdom, riches, and a long life (1 Kings 3:11-15). Solomon ruled for forty years and had many great achievements. He displayed great wisdom in many things, so much so that the Queen of Sheba went to visit him and see this wisdom for herself (1 Kings 10 and 2 Chronicles 9). According to the Bible, she was impressed.

Solomon was supposedly the wisest man who ever lived, but he was also the most foolish because he chose to ignore God's commandments in several ways. When he instructed his sons, he spoke about both wisdom and foolishness from experience. Forgetfulness and ignorance have no place with wisdom and understanding.

Father, please give me wisdom. Alert my consciousness when I'm forgetting your Word. Help me keep wisdom in my heart to guide and protect me.

Love Wisdom

Do not forsake wisdom, and she will protect you;
love her, and she will watch over you.
Proverbs 4:6 NIV

Wisdom in the Bible specifically refers to God's Word. There is no truth, love, or wisdom outside of God. He is the pure source of them all. If you forsake wisdom, you forsake God. If you love wisdom, you love God. Since God has created, defined, and acknowledged wisdom as the best path through life, we must go to him to learn it.

Proverbs is the collection of thoughts by King Solomon about wisdom. God blessed Solomon with wisdom, so his words are worthy of our attention. Read and contemplate the lessons of Solomon. Don't forget or forsake them; knowledge of them will protect you. Pursue the learning of wisdom as an act of love.

Dear God, open my eyes to your wisdom in these pages. Help me hear and take the messages into my heart. May I always remember what I have learned from you.

Get Wisdom

The beginning of wisdom is this: Get wisdom.
Though it cost all you have, get understanding.
PROVERBS 4:7 NIV

Have you ever thought about what the pursuit of wisdom might cost you? Since wisdom only comes from God, only by seeking God do we grow in wisdom. If we spend time seeking God, that's time spent not seeking something else. What activity in your life might need to take a backseat? You could spend your entire life seeking of God, and it would be a life well spent.

Whatever it may cost us in time or fortitude, pursuing God and growing in wisdom is worth it. There are no riches more worthy of our ambition. A wise person understands the worth of wisdom. More than knowledge, common sense, intuition, or raw intelligence, wisdom understands what the heart of God desires. There is nothing of greater value than that.

Holy Father, you are wise and understanding. Your ways and wisdom are infinitely greater than mine. Your words encourage me, and the time I spend with you strengthens and inspires me.

Embrace Wisdom

"Prize her highly, and she will exalt you;
she will honor you if you embrace her."
PROVERBS 4:8 ESV

The return on investment with wisdom is clearly outlined in our verse today. Prize it, and you will be exalted. If you value the wisdom you gain by learning the Word, you will be lifted up. You will reap the benefits of being wise by making good decisions, having a good reputation, and being respected. If you embrace your time with the Word, you will become honorable in your character and overall behavior. It's a more than fair return!

To some extent, we seek the approval of others. By the teenage years, for instance, peers have replaced parents as the most influential group in children's lives. God rises above all influence by instructing believers, young and old alike, to seek his wisdom as the highest authority and greatest approval.

Keep me close to you, my Father, so I may learn from you. Keep me in your sights so I may feel your direction and learn your wisdom.

Every word of God proves true;
he is a shield to those who
take refuge in him.

Proverbs 30:5 esv

Deliver a Crown

"She will place on your head an ornament of grace;
A crown of glory she will deliver to you."
PROVERBS 4:9 NKJV

Glory is not a common word these days. It entails more familiar words like honor and praise, but it's more than that. Glory raises these traits to a level of distinction. It raises the person who possesses wisdom above the rest. That is why a crown is delivered; that is why grace is placed as an ornament on your head. You are to be distinguished above the others. Your wise behavior is acknowledged as beautiful, desirable, and wonderful.

The crown is meant for royalty, but the only thing royal about us is our relationship to God. Because he is King, and because we are grafted in as sons and daughters of the King, we are also royal. It speaks well of us if we behave in a manner worthy of our Father, the King.

My Father and King, may I seek your Word and spend the time I need to know you and learn to be wise. May the crown of glory I desire sit on my head as a testimony to you.

My Child

My child, listen to me and do as I say,
and you will have a long, good life.
PROVERBS 4:10 NLT

For those of us who are or have been parents to young children, these are familiar words! We demand our children to pay attention to what we say. We can't miss the point here; wisdom is something mature Christians actively grow toward, and unbelievers and young Christians must heed lessons to learn it. The reward is uplifting: pay attention and have a good, long life. Read the Word and learn God's wisdom, and there are blessings ahead for you.

The growth patterns of a child's character can teach us something. They aren't born with an inherent ability to recognize wise decisions. They are exposed repeatedly, by their parents and teachers, to what is wise. The child's intelligence may factor into this development, but often it is simply the amount of time invested in guidance and teaching that does the work. Spend the time, dear Christian, with your heavenly Father, who teaches and guides us perfectly.

Dear God, open my eyes and ears to your wisdom. Teach and guide me as I seek you.

Instructed and Led

I have instructed you in the way of wisdom;
I have led you in upright paths.
PROVERBS 4:11 NASB

God is the perfect teacher and guide. The path to wisdom is in his Word and his presence through prayer. He assures us this beautiful blessing is available to us forever, and his promises stand forever. May we soak our souls in his instruction and absorb directly from his Word. Let us trust him so much we can see, feel, and know what he wants for us.

God doesn't impose himself on us. He opens the door for us to learn from all he has made available. We may choose to follow him, be instructed by his Word, and follow the narrow path set before us, but we can also choose to turn away. If we are willing to walk through that door, he is willing to instruct us in the way of wisdom and lead us along the upright path.

Jesus, you are my heart's desire. May I open the door of my heart to you alone. Help me hear the voice of the Father as he teaches and leads me toward everlasting life with you.

Balance

When you walk, you won't be held back;
when you run, you won't stumble.
PROVERBS 4:12 NLT

Protection from faltering is more poignant as we get older, but it's important for the very young as well. Many people seek a doctor for help with balance. God is speaking spiritually here; our bodies will falter and fail, but our spirits are in his hands if we so choose. Having good balance means being able to control your body's uprightness which is key to not stumbling. Having the ability to not stumble spiritually is important if we want to grow in the Lord. Wisdom is acquired by spending time with the Lord in the Word.

The overlapping meanings between the physical and the spiritual in the Word are useful tools for us to understand God. Stumbling spiritually leads to embarrassment and grief. Stumbling physically leads to embarrassment and pain. Stay close to the Word and allow him to teach you his wisdom.

Father God, open my heart to your wisdom. Allow me to be a testimony to a life well lived.

Instructions

Hold on to instruction, do not let it go;
guard it well, for it is your life.
PROVERBS 4:13 NIV

God tells us we can access instruction on wisdom in his Word; we need only open the pages of the Bible and read. The power of his Word will be immediately apparent, but the power of his Word over time is even more impactful. We change and grow as he spends time with us. We become purer forms of ourselves, and this is evident in the way we live.

Clinging to the Word is a novel concept for a new believer. What does it really mean? Opening the Bible and eagerly seeking a new message from God each day is a joy. It's a way for us to learn about the Creator of the entire universe. We seek instruction and a guiding hand, and God delivers. He wants each of us to know his Word so we can better know his intentions for our lives.

Dear Lord, open your Word to me so I can understand and discern the path you intend for me.

What You Learned

Remember what you have been taught,
and don't let go of it.
Keep all that you have learned;
it is the most important thing in life.
PROVERBS 4:13 NCV

Forgetfulness is the bane of humanity, yet committing the Word to our hearts and remembering it has strength not found in any other experience. The name of Joseph's oldest son, Manasseh, means "God has made me forget" (Genesis 41:51). There are some things that God wants us to forget, like past grievances or the sins of others against us, but in today's verse, God tells us to remember. Remember all you have learned because it is the most important thing in life.

Investing in regular and purposeful reading of the Word may be the most important thing you do because God says to remember it, and we can't remember what we haven't learned yet. Make the effort to learn so you can remember.

Dear Father, keep me close so I may learn. Help me remember all you have taught me.

Light of Dawn

The way of the good person is like the light of dawn,
growing brighter and brighter until full daylight.
PROVERBS 4:18 NCV

Because the sun never goes away—it is always evident somewhere on earth—the process of the sun getting brighter from dawn to day is an issue of where you are standing. If we understand that the path from dawn to day is marked by a growing brightness, we then can understand that the path from sin to wisdom is similar. We need to grow toward the increasing light. We need to seek wisdom to understand the exposing brightness of truth and grace.

Living in full daylight is a blessing. It means we are fully in the presence of God's redeeming truth. We have nothing to hide; we have nothing left to reveal because we live in the light. It is an amazing blessing and relief to live like this. The goal isn't to be a good person. The goal is to live within the confines of God's amazing path: the enlightened life and the way everlasting.

Dear God, may I see clearly the way you have set for me. May I be the person you want me to be and live in a way that displays the growing light.

Pay Attention

Give attention to my words;
Incline your ear to my sayings.
Do not let them depart from your eyes;
Keep them in the midst of your heart.
PROVERBS 4:20-21 NKJV

Which voices are you heeding? Who influences you? The course of your life is directly aligned with who holds your attention. Are the things you're putting before your eyes and ears positive influences? Taking time to block out the noise and listen to God is essential in our hectic, fast-paced world. God may be speaking, but are we listening? Are we even able to hear? It is important to deliberately step away from social media, the news, friends, music, and any noise other than the sweet voice of our Savior.

Let's give our attention to God first and foremost. To incline our ears means we have to lean in and listen. God's words deserve a permanent spot on our hearts, in our ears, and before our eyes. There are so many voices vying for our attention, but only one voice deserves our full devotion.

What do you want to say to me today, Lord? I will take the time to find silence and listen. I will listen to your voice first.

Spilling Over

Above all else, guard your heart,
for everything you do flows from it.
PROVERBS 4:23 NIV

We must be careful what we invite into our hearts. We can't hide the contents of our hearts for long because words and actions seep out from them. As children of God, we need to live intentionally. God has a purpose for us, and when we allow ungodly influences into our hearts, they distort our purposes and cloud our judgment.

Let's take time to tend our hearts and be filled with God's love, joy, and generosity. These are the attributes fitting for children of God. What if kindness, peace, and hope flowed from our hearts into our actions and words? What sort of impact would that have on those around us?

Lord, guard my heart. I want to be so full of your joy, love, and mercy that they spill out on everyone around me. Keep me free from influences that try to tell me I should only be concerned with my happiness. I want more than happiness, God; I want holiness.

Listen to Wisdom

My son, pay attention to my wisdom,
Incline your ear to my understanding.
PROVERBS 5:1 NASB

Wisdom is meant to be shared. In Proverbs, we see chapters written by a father to his son. He beseeches his son to pay attention to the lessons that took him a lifetime to learn. Proverbs repeatedly states that a wise person listens to such lessons while a fool does not.

To gain wisdom, we don't just need to read Scripture and do the best we can to be good Christians; we need to listen to the people in our lives who have valuable guidance to share from their experiences. It's important to seek counsel from wise and godly people so we can grow, not just through the wisdom God reveals directly to us, but also through what he has revealed to others.

God, thank you for giving me access to your Word. Please make me more discerning so I can share your wisdom with others and learn from those who are wiser than I am.

I'm Not Enough

She does not ponder the path of life;
Her ways are unstable, she does not know it.
PROVERBS 5:6 NASB

The hardest people to reach are those who don't know they're in trouble. Where there is no knowledge of a shortcoming, it will never be rectified. A Christian's first order of business is to admit their need for a savior; they recognize they can't earn salvation and are entirely dependent on the mercy of God to be rid of sin.

When we ponder the path of life and consider what it means to live for the glory of God, we come to the realization that we don't have what it takes to do that on our own. This realization leads us to seek Christ and follow him. Rather than causing despair, this knowledge should spur us to release our insufficiencies to God so he can use them to display his holiness to the rest of the world.

Lord, only by your grace have I realized I am not enough on my own. Thank you for opening my eyes to my lack of perfection so I can pursue yours. You have freed me from my limited humanity and made me part of an eternal story.

Choosing the Hard Path

Listen to me
And do not depart from the words of my mouth.
PROVERBS 5:7 NASB

It's hard to do the right thing. In each moment of temptation, the sinful nature recoils at the idea of denying itself pleasure. It's not natural for a human to follow wisdom. If we have a desire to follow Jesus and hate sin, we have to know its destructive power, how God feels about it, and what instruction he has given us to overcome it.

The more we read the Bible and learn about the character of God, the more we are empowered to love what he loves and hate what he hates. When we see what sin does to people and glimpse the restorative power of God's authority, we will be better equipped to hold fast to his instructions.

God, I ask humbly for a heart desperate to know you. I am hopeless to do good on my own. Please teach me to see the bigger picture when I am tempted. Show me the death that giving in to sin will bring and strengthen me to choose the righteous path.

Committed Love

Let your wife be a fountain of blessing for you.
Rejoice in the wife of your youth.
May you always be captivated by her love.
PROVERBS 5:18-19 NLT

Isaiah 62:5 compares the joy a bridegroom feels about his bride to how God rejoices over his people. There is no doubt we were made for relationships. Whatever relationships you have in your life—parents, spouse, children, friends, coworkers, neighbors—cherish them. Solomon advised his students to have joy in their relationships and to remember their commitments.

We live in an age of instant gratification. We don't like waiting for our food, on hold, in lines, or for a package to come in the mail. If things don't happen the way we want, when we want them, we're likely to bail and find something or someone else. There are good reasons to leave an unhealthy relationship or work environment, but let's not jump to that conclusion without good cause. Anything or anyone worthwhile is going to require work. We can rejoice in that and stick with our commitments.

Heavenly Father, please teach me to love the way you love. Help me stay true to my commitments.

Fully Known and Loved

The ways of a man are before the eyes of the LORD,
And He watches all his paths.
PROVERBS 5:21 NASB

Integrity is doing what's right even when no one is looking. As Christians, we know God sees everything we do and knows why we do things. He knows our most secret thoughts. Our selfish choices and failures to resist temptation are on display to the one who tests hearts. No one knows the depravity of a human heart like the Lord, yet no one loves like the Lord does.

Despite our mistakes and rejection of his good plan, God made a way for us to be with him forever. He loves us so much; he was willing to sacrifice Jesus to close the chasm we made between ourselves and God. Our great joy is to know the Lord sees all our thoughts while still loving, guiding, and interceding for us.

Father, you see all and know all, yet you love me. I will never understand this mystery, but I thank you for its reality. I don't deserve the mercy you offer, but I gratefully receive it and give all the glory to you.

Promising to Pay

Be careful about giving a guarantee for somebody else's loan, about promising to pay what someone else owes.
Proverbs 6:1 NCV

There's plenty of worldly advice about lending money, and the Bible also covers the topic. Great care must be made before you give someone money. This verse specifically addresses the issue of promising to pay someone's debt.

It is good to support others during challenging times (James 1:27), to give people a fair wage (Matthew 20:1-5), and even to give money without the expectation of repayment (Luke 6:30). In every case, you put no requirement upon them nor impose a burden the recipient cannot meet. Giving someone money to relieve their debt is a specific issue.

Lord, you know what is best for me; your Word is perfect and holy. If someone asks me to pay their debt, it's wise to follow your advice. May I learn about you through this lesson and learn to trust you with larger issues.

Go to the Ant

Go to the ant, you sluggard;
consider its ways and be wise!
PROVERBS 6:6 NIV

The ant is upheld in this proverb as a high standard of character and behavior. That might be surprising, but God created both people and ants, so learning about the ant is a worthy pursuit! Ants are very industrious and work hard for their homes. Ants are also social creatures and live their whole lives in highly structured communities.

Working in groups is one of the ways they adapt to new challenges and threats to their communities. They work and travel together. They communicate with each other and hunt for prey together. Believers will be wise to notice the ways of the ant because of these and other characteristics.

Dear Father, thank you for your Word which guides us toward behaviors and characteristics that edify you. May I live wisely and emulate the behaviors you tell us are important.

No Leader

Ants have no commander, no leader or ruler.
PROVERBS 6:7 NCV

The largest known ant colony in the world stretches 3,700 miles from northern Italy through the south of France and along to the Atlantic coast in Spain. This is a relatively young colony because the ant species, the Argentine, was only introduced to Europe about eighty years ago. The most noteworthy characteristic of ant colonies is that they have no leaders, so they are self-organized. They communicate clearly and work constantly together toward the building and maintenance of their colonies. 3,700 miles is a long line of community!

Could Christians organize and function as a unified whole to build community? Maybe sin will always interfere in our efforts, but we are told to seek the Lord's guidance and emulate his path for community and fellowship. Each ant is driven to work, but they also work alongside each other in a specific locale. We can't personally take responsibility for the whole world; that rests upon our Creator.

Father God, give me the drive to do your will. Let me know what you want me to do with my day.

Summertime

They labor hard all summer,
gathering food for the winter.
PROVERBS 6:8 NLT

Although evolutionists say humans were first hunter-gatherers and then eventually farmers, the Bible says Cain, the son of Adam and Eve, was a farmer. Growing food has been a part of all human history, but people have hunted and foraged throughout time as well. Finding and growing food is a big part of life, and where there is winter, preserving food before it is hard to grow, forage, or hunt is essential. Those who don't stock up for winter will go hungry.

Because ants are cold-blooded, they grow sluggish in the winter. They huddle together for protection and live off their stored food. Harvester ants collect seeds and store them in chambers called granaries. Honeypot ants, also called storage ants, store liquids in their stomachs. This is available when it is needed by other ants. Leafcutter ants cut pieces of leaves to feed a fungus in their nests as a type of winter farm. When we live in a time of plenty, it is biblical to set aside and prepare for times of hardship.

Dear Lord, may I be aware of times when I should prepare for hardships and challenges. Open my eyes for opportunities to gather.

Arise from Sleep

How long will you lie there, O sluggard?
When will you arise from your sleep?
PROVERBS 6:9 ESV

Laziness is not an admirable trait. The Bible instructs all believers to be workers for the kingdom. We do not get to live a lethargic life because we live in the age of grace. However, laziness is not the same as rest. There are both sabbath rests, which are usually about a day per week, and sabbatical rests, which are less often but for a longer period.

Proverbs has many teachings about the sluggard, and the verse 26:16 may offer the best definition: "The sluggard is wiser in his own eyes than seven men who can answer sensibly." Rest and laziness are not the same thing. Please give yourself the appropriate rest, dear believer, and when it is over, work for the kingdom again.

Dear Jesus, please forgive me when I am lazy. Help me recognize when I could be doing something for you rather than indulging in time-wasting pursuits. Please make me aware of days or seasons of rest and allow me to rejuvenate without guilt.

Like a Drifter

"A little sleep, a little slumber,
A little folding of the hands to rest,"
Then your poverty will come in like a drifter,
And your need like an armed man.
PROVERBS 6:10-11 NASB

That word *drifter* is translated in other versions as robber, bandit, traveler, vagabond, thief, and plunderer. The phrase *armed man*, however, is pretty much the same throughout versions. You can see with the drifter translations that it was a challenge to get that word right, and all the translations together might be the best way to understand the gist of the meaning.

If you forfeit the time given to you, if you choose to lay around and not be productive, you will be poor. You'll live in poverty, be it spiritual or financial, and slowly, over the course of months or years, your choice or lack of engagement will rob you of purpose and joy. You won't have your needs met, but maybe more importantly, you won't know what the will of God is for your life. You will miss it by choosing laziness instead.

Father, open my eyes to your opportunities. Give me a zest for life that can only come from you.

A Scoundrel

A worthless person, a wicked man
goes around speaking dishonestly.
PROVERBS 6:12 CSB

A scoundrel is worthless, lawless, and without a yoke. They are given to corruption and rebellion. This word occurs twenty-six times in the Old Testament, and it refers to people who coerce others toward false gods, speak against the one true God, or indulge themselves at the cost of their responsibilities. The sons of Eli, the prophet in 1 Samuel, for instance, were called worthless because they were sleeping with various women and misusing the sacrificed meat. Lying, which is noted in our verse today, is a noteworthy sign of a scoundrel. Eli's sons started on their paths of corruption by speaking words that defied the Lord.

2 Timothy 3:16-17 tells us that the Word is intended "for teaching, for reproof, for correction, and for training in righteousness, so that the man of God may be complete, equipped for every good work." God doesn't leave anything to chance. He fills in all the blanks as to what is good and what is evil.

Lord, steer me away from a perverse tongue and open my eyes to the beauty of your truth. Allow me to see you and bask in your glory.

The Lord Hates

There are six things the LORD hates, seven that are detestable to him:
haughty eyes, a lying tongue, hands that shed innocent blood,
a heart that devises wicked schemes,
feet that are quick to rush into evil,
a false witness who pours out lies
and a person who stirs up conflict in the community.
PROVERBS 6:16-19 NIV

If you were wondering what God hates, here is your list. The false witness who discredits another person is at the top. Lovers of God speak truthfully when they are called upon to witness. The dissenter or manipulator is the second trait. This leads to the third: a heart that plans wicked things can't love the world. When we think about feet that are quick to run to evil, it's easy to consider the nosy neighbor who rushes out with gossip and pursues it.

When God speaks to Job, he's brutal about the proud. There won't be a lot of grace for unrepentant, prideful people. God is passionate about righteousness especially for the innocent. No person is without sin, yet those who seek him and repent are lifted up.

Dear Lord, keep me from those things that you hate. I want to emulate your love in everything I do.

Parental Guidance

My son, keep your father's commandment,
and forsake not your mother's teaching.
Bind them on your heart always; tie them around your neck.
PROVERBS 6:20-21 ESV

Even those with unbelieving, sin-driven parents can, with wisdom and time, discern nuggets of truth and beauty in the way they were brought up. God can leak into the hearts of parents for the sake of the children. God is a loving God, and the lessons we take with us into adult life don't have to be all about the negatives of our upbringing. The heart of God can override the bad memories and give believers grace for those who raised them. We can see the life lessons when we look back. We can see the hand of God where once we would only see horrors.

Every person is born into sin, but the teachings and rules of our parents can reflect the heart of God. Even if the teachings are a mess and the rules are based in selfishness, God can and will use those details to bring us into the kingdom, and our stories can bring others with us.

Dear Father, let me see my earthly parents with your eyes as your vessels for lessons and learning as I was growing up.

When You Awake

When you walk, they will guide you;
when you sleep, they will watch over you;
when you awake, they will speak to you.
PROVERBS 6:22 NIV

Parental impact on a child's growth can't be underestimated. Whether mother and father are aware of it or not, they become a child's default thoughts often through adulthood. If these lifelong lessons are of God, they are a balm to the soul. If they are more worldly in their intent, they can still guide in unexpected ways.

God walks with his children no matter their age, and as our Father, he guides and directs us lovingly toward the path he has chosen for us. God has given us his Holy Spirit to dwell us no matter what we are experiencing. No matter where we are, there he is too. What a blessing to know God has put us where we will be protected and guided. He has determined our families, both the ones we were given as children as well as the ones we have as adults. We will hear those guiding voices because of his direction.

Lord God, you are almighty and the one I love. Thank you for all the teaching and rules I had growing up. I know you use them for my protection.

Teaching Is a Light

These commands are like a lamp;
this teaching is like a light.
And the correction that comes from them
will help you have life.
PROVERBS 6:23 NCV

Psalm 119:105 famously says, “Your word is a lamp for my feet and a light for my path.” The lamp in Psalms and the commands in today’s verse provide an interesting study. God’s Word, through the commands of our parents, provides direction for our feet. In other words, our next steps can be discerned by God’s Word in the rules our parents laid out for us. We know how to make decisions because we grew up with rules and because God’s Word offers the right commandments for us to follow.

The correction and discipline we received from our parents and God’s Word provides overall enlightenment in our lives that will keep us from evil and allow us to find wisdom. We can’t escape darkness without God’s Word, and our parents’ teachings are a natural vessel the Lord uses.

Lord, open my eyes to the lessons and teachings handed down to me from my parents. Help me use them to light my life’s path.

Rhetorical Question

Can a man scoop a flame into his lap and not have his clothes catch on fire?
PROVERBS 6:27 NLT

Sin, like a flame, can grow out of control quickly. It starts out small but gets to a point where it can't be controlled. If we keep in mind that sin is often clothed as temptation or selfishness, we can learn how to be alert to the little flame before it becomes a consuming fire. James 1:14-15 says, "Temptation comes from our own desires, which entice us and drag us away. These desires give birth to sinful actions. And when sin is allowed to grow, it gives birth to death." That is not the direction we want to go!

The good news is you serve the loving God. He has redeemed you through the blood of his perfect Son, and at any point during a fire of sin, you can turn to him and be brought back from death. May the God and Father of our Lord Jesus Christ "give you spiritual wisdom and insight so that you might grow in your knowledge of God" (Ephesians 1:17).

Dear Jesus, take my heart and my whole life too. Keep me alert to the little flames of sin in my life so the only consuming fire I experience is my love for you.

Treasure His Commands

Follow my advice, my son;
always treasure my commands.
PROVERBS 7:1 NLT

The Lord loves us so much, he gave us instructions for living. He told us to treasure those commands so we would know he understands what is best for us. If we love him as well, we will put his words above our inclinations. Christians need to give their wills over to God because his wisdom and love overrides human shortsightedness and sinful nature.

We can learn to submit to God by reading his Word. It's difficult for us to give up our strong inclinations, but as we read the wisdom in the pages of the Bible, our hearts soften, and the Holy Spirit moves. Our eyes open to the grace of God, and we become his children through the seed planted by the Spirit. Then we are capable of following God's advice and treasuring his commands.

Lord, teach me your Word. Give me grace so I can see your truth and grow in your wisdom.

Keep His Commands

Keep my commands and you will live;
guard my teachings as the apple of your eye.
Bind them on your fingers;
write them on the tablet of your heart.
PROVERBS 7:2-3 NIV

Our eyes see beauty and loveliness. Our fingers are front and center in our work. Our hearts record the events of our lives. When we follow God's commands, we determine the path of our lives. God tells us to see the beauty in his instructions, the applicability of his work, and the life-changing ability of his Word living within our hearts. At every point, our lives are blessed and crafted by his wonder when we submit to him.

God made his commands beautiful. Submitting to God's Word is submitting to him. He cherishes our obedience and gives us grace when we embrace his wisdom in our daily lives. We honor God when we take his commands into our hearts and obediently follow them. This results in life for us: an eternal, everlasting, amazing life spent in the presence of the one true King.

Father, please give me your presence so I can know you. Set your commands deeply into my heart so I can be obedient.

Seductive Flattery

Say to wisdom, "You are my sister,"
And call understanding your nearest kin,
That they may keep you from the immoral woman,
From the seductress who flatters with her words.
PROVERBS 7:4-5 NKJV

We need to keep God's wisdom close like a sister. She is someone we know and trust. She loves us and keeps us safe in all she tells us to do. She protects us because she loves us with her whole heart. We are safe with her advice; we are protected with her words.

The woman who speaks sweet, empty words can't be trusted. She tells us things that make us feel good in the moment but harm us over time. We are led down a path of self-absorption and indulgence. Flattery is never used by the wise; it is a tool of the deceiver. It is prudent to heed God when he tells us to avoid this woman but trust our sister.

God, I know you and love you. I love your Word, and I love your advice. Please keep me wary of the deceiver and his flattering words. Keep me close to you so I can discern.

Two Women

Let not your heart turn aside to her ways;
do not stray into her paths.
PROVERBS 7:25 ESV

There are drastic differences between the adulterous woman portrayed in Proverbs 7 and the noble woman depicted in Proverbs 31. The former leads her victims to their destruction, whereas the latter brings her husband and entire household honor and provision. The Proverbs 7 woman seeks only her own gratification and does not care about who she hurts; the Proverbs 31 woman works hard to care for those she loves.

We get to choose which woman to model our lives after. We choose which woman we align with. Since God designed our hearts and created them to find full satisfaction only in him, any endeavors to find satisfaction in the world will lead to disappointment and emptiness. When we lose ourselves in loving service to God and others, we find ourselves, our purpose, and our satisfaction.

Oh God, I want my words and actions to bring blessing to others and not curses. I want to bring honor to you and encouragement to those I love. Help me choose the more noble way even when temptation whispers.

Understanding's Voice

Listen as Wisdom calls out!
Hear as understanding raises her voice!
PROVERBS 8:1 NLT

Unlike the noisy gong or the clanging symbol, when Wisdom calls out, she has a compelling voice. Christians are drawn to her because she has the voice of God himself, and the wisdom of God is driven by his love. 1 Corinthians 13, the love chapter, tells us all the languages of the earth and the angels are fruitless and useless without love. Anything we do, say, or think is fruitless without love.

Wisdom and love are the outpouring of the Holy Spirit in our lives. We know we are in the presence of the Almighty God as we speak words that compel us toward God. We know the Holy Spirit is working through us when we allow understanding and love to take over our thoughts, so we bless others rather than reject them. God moves his beautiful Word through us in wisdom, understanding, and love.

Father, break me so I can hear your voice. Speak through me and allow me to give wisdom and understanding to others.

April

The fear of the Lord
is the beginning of wisdom,
and the knowledge of the Holy One
is insight.

Proverbs 9:10 ESV

Excellent Things

Listen, for I will speak of excellent things,
And from the opening of my lips will come right things.
PROVERBS 8:6 NKJV

Perfection, beauty, purity, and grandeur are of the Lord. His way is excellent, and his path is wonderful. His Words speak of the best way to live and the way to eternity with him. When we follow God and believe the Bible, we merge with him. We give ourselves over to the perfection and purity that is him. We transform because our minds are renewed.

As we are made new again in Christ, our hearts and demeanors change, and we diverge from the path which lead to our demise. We instead take the high road; we are heaven-bound and glory-bent. What was dead is now alive, and what comes out of our mouths is now right. We no longer speak in a way that leads to death. We are one with the Holy Spirit, and his way is life everlasting.

Lord, forgive me for my many sins. Please redeem me so my sins are forgiven. Lead me in your way everlasting so my mouth will speak righteousness.

Silver nor Gold

"Choose my instruction rather than silver,
and knowledge rather than pure gold."
PROVERBS 8:10 NLT

The most precious metals, owned by the wealthiest people with the most luxurious things and the most comfortable lives, are nothing, absolutely nothing, when compared to the glory that is ours in Christ. The Lord has given us his Word and paved the way to knowledge in him. He didn't leave anything to chance when he recorded his commandments. He wasn't waffling when he said the only way to heaven is through Jesus Christ (John 14:5).

Clear instructions leave us with a solid knowledge of God's expectations. He lofts his instructions over the value of precious metals, so we needn't guess or misunderstand how truly valuable God's Word is. We are told to choose him. We are told to love his instructions and knowledge. He has given this precious treasure to everyone who believes.

Lord, I believe. I give my life to you, and I love your commandments. Thank you for clarity and beauty in your Word.

Wisdom Plus Prudence

"I, wisdom, dwell together with prudence;
I possess knowledge and discretion."
PROVERBS 8:12 NIV

Wisdom lives with prudence, and it owns knowledge and discretion. It's an interesting picture in today's proverb. If we imagine wisdom as a person, it's logical that prudence is a partner. Prudence gives believers reservation and temperance. It slows reactions down and increases prayer and tapping into the Holy Spirit. We leave room for God's voice, and that requires space to think before responding. That takes wisdom and prudence.

God blesses his children when they pursue him and his Word. He blesses us with insight, knowledge, and an ability to discern good from evil. He equips us to be prepared for the next conversation or the next kindness. We gain insight into the way people think or what they need. We become vessels for the Holy Spirit to move in this world and call his people to himself.

Lord, I am so excited to be a vessel for your Holy Spirit. I'm grateful to belong to your family.

Hate Evil

"If you respect the LORD, you will also hate evil.
I hate pride and bragging,
evil ways and lies."
PROVERBS 8:13 NCV

It's funny how we change when we repent of our sins and follow the Lord. We become what we used to hate, and we hate what we used to be. It's a complete flip. The ways of the world conflict with those who follow the ways of God. We no longer focus on earthly pleasures; we are now pursuing treasures in heaven.

Christians grow as by praying and reading the Bible. As we do this, the Holy Spirit moves into our hearts and convicts us of righteousness. We become God's children and think his thoughts. We hate evil and all its ways. We hate pride; we hate lies and bragging. We hate ourselves if we sin in these ways. Then we repent, truly repent, and move on with a fresh, appreciated forgiveness.

Lord, as I become more like you, please keep me from the sins I hate so much. Purify me and keep me in your way.

Mutual Love

"I will show my love to those who passionately love me.
For they will search and search continually until they find me."
PROVERBS 8:17 TPT

Have you spent time and effort searching for God this week? Like any of us, God wants a mutual relationship and not one where the effort is one-sided. He wants us to search for him, yearn for him, and miss him when we haven't spent time with him. He wants us to be excited about everything he intends to show us. He wants to actively participate in our lives and not just as a fallback for tough times.

Have you experienced God's love? Great! There is more to experience. The Lord is always ready to show us more and captivate us with his greatness. Let's love him passionately and purposefully. May we make it our mission to cherish our mutual relationship with him.

I love you passionately, dear God, and I will never stop pursuing you. You are my deepest desire, and nothing compares to the joy I feel because of our relationship. Thank you for everything you have and will share with me. I am excited to walk through this life with you.

Paths of Justice

"I walk in righteousness,
in paths of justice."
PROVERBS 8:20 NLT

Righteousness and justice are beautiful things, yet the world seems to be bypassing them altogether. We see injustices daily around us and in the news. We constantly hear of unrighteousness, and it can be overwhelming and discouraging.

Christians can do one thing in the face of evil: walk according to God's ways. His ways are righteous, and his path is just. We rest in the security and knowledge that God has won the war already and we are destined to be with him in glory. There, perfect justice rules. Perfect righteousness undergirds all of eternity. We serve a pure king who loves completely. We are protected by his Word, and he declares us holy through the blood of his Son.

Thank you for your sacrifice, oh God. Thank you for your perfect plan for our preservation in your eternal home with you.

Wisdom with God

"I, wisdom, was with the Lord when he began his work, long before he made anything else."
Proverbs 8:22 NCV

God and wisdom were both at the beginning. We can't separate God from wisdom or wisdom from God. We can't deny that all wisdom is God's; it was with him from the beginning and long before he created the earth and us. He, with the Holy Spirit and the Son, existed together with wisdom before the world began.

We serve this amazing God. We are products of his glorious and creative mind and exist by the compelling wonder of his will. We bless him with our love, loyalty, and obedience. It's an honor to serve the great and wonderful God who cares about every hair on our heads and every motive of our hearts.

Lord, thank you for forgiving me for my sins and for taking me to heaven to live with you. I am honored to serve you all the days of my life.

Earth's Foundation

"I was there when he ordered the sea
not to go beyond the borders he had set.
I was there when he laid the earth's foundation."
PROVERBS 8:29 NCV

With wisdom by his side, God constructed the planet. We are right to be awed by this. It's jaw-dropping to comprehend the ways of God throughout creation, but the steps of creation are literally amazing. In the Word, we have insight into our processes and purpose. The borders of the sea were set by order of the Almighty, and wisdom was there. The foundations of the earth were laid. Wisdom was there.

Wisdom is a force. It's with God from forever and is ours to learn by following and knowing him. Without wisdom, we are missing the Lord himself. Pursuing God brings wisdom into the relationship.

Lord, I need you and love you. I have nothing to offer but your own creation: myself. Make me and mold me into your image.

Wisdom Rejoices

"I was constantly at his side.
I was filled with delight day after day,
rejoicing always in his presence,
rejoicing in his whole world
and delighting in mankind."
PROVERBS 8:30-31 NIV

Earlier in verse twenty-two, Wisdom declared she was "the first of [the Lord's] works." In today's Scripture, she was *constantly* at God's side and *filled with delight day after day*. Now, she rejoices in his creation and specifically humankind.

Our beautiful world is not random or accidental; it is planned, orderly, and intermingled with wisdom. God, in his infinite understanding, created us according to his flawless plan and placed us in this stunning landscape. Although humanity has brought a lot of hate and destruction to our planet, God's mission is still in motion, and he's perfectly putting all pieces in place. Can you see it? Do you recognize his handiwork all around you?

Nature declares your glory, oh God! I see it in the changing seasons, the mountains and oceans, the sunrises and sunsets. Everywhere I look, I see your creativity, and I wonder at your majesty.

Wait by the Door

"Blessed is the one who listens to me,
watching daily at my gates,
waiting beside my doors."
PROVERBS 8:34 ESV

Walking with the Lord isn't a one-and-done activity. It's a lifelong commitment that needs constant communication and moment-by-moment loyalty. God is a jealous god, and he wants nothing to interfere with our relationship with him. There are a few things we can concretely do to keep God first in our lives.

The only way to hear God's instructions is to be in his Word. We need to read or listen daily to learn what he has to say. We also need to take him seriously when he tells us to watch daily at the gates. Nothing compares to daily time with our Maker to keep our priorities straight. The voice of the Lord draws us in, so we want more of him when we have even a little bit, and this leads to the last point in today's proverb. Wait on God. Wait at his door and wait for him to speak. He will. He has things to tell us, ways to motivate us, and love to pour into us. We are his beloved.

God, I love to hear from you and learn from you. I am overwhelmed by your love for me, yet I seek it more and more.

Don't Love Death

"Whoever finds me finds life
and obtains favor from the LORD,
but he who fails to find me injures himself;
all who hate me love death."
PROVERBS 8:35-36 ESV

In his wisdom, God delineates life and death for us in the Bible and throughout Proverbs. We need to find God; then we find life and God's favor. We seek the Father, and having found him, we are blessed with everlasting life. God loves our pursuit of him because he also seeks us. He pursues us with stubborn love. When we join his family, he showers us with blessings and love in ways we could not understand before we knew him.

It's self-defeating to deny God. We deny the true purpose of our existence if we don't observe God's role in creating us. He made us; he formed our purpose; he knows every detail of what we need and what fulfills us for a life in eternity.

God, I love seeing your way at work in me. I love that you are forever in my life and that you sought me for eternal purposes.

Wisdom Personified

Wisdom has built her house,
She has hewn out her seven pillars.
PROVERBS 9:1 NKJV

Wisdom, personified here as a woman, has built a house for herself with seven pillars. Seven is the number of completeness and perfection in the Bible, so these seven pillars could mean that the house is in order and finished. It could also show that the house is well-supported and strong. A person could really delve into this verse's meaning. For instance, wisdom was present at the beginning of time as God's first acquisition in Proverbs 8:22. God then created the world in how many days? Seven. It's fun to contemplate God's perfection on different levels.

As we mature spiritually through age and stages of life, and we find deeper levels of understanding in the Bible as we read. It's interesting to think about the house as just a house. It's also interesting to think about Wisdom's house as an allegory for the creation of the world or the maturity of a believer's heart. God could very well mean every one of these explanations for this proverb.

Dear Father, open my heart and mind to the messages in your Word and in Proverbs 9. May I see your wisdom and learn from you.

Accepting Rebuke

Do not rebuke mockers or they will hate you;
rebuke the wise and they will love you.
PROVERBS 9:8 NIV

How can you tell a wise person from a foolish one? Watch how they respond to correction. Some people are unwilling to listen to constructive criticism or loving rebuke. They care more about their pride and image than the truth. They don't want to improve or correct themselves; they want to feel good and avoid feeling bad. These people cower in the face of confrontation and are not up to the challenge of becoming better.

Save your correction for those who are willing to accept it, for they will love and appreciate you because you made the effort to help them grow. Those people are worth your rebuke, and they will continue to great heights. Keep your heart humble toward those willing to help you grow and learn. Accept rebuke from the wise. Accept discipline from God. In time, you will grow wiser still.

Lord, I don't want to be a mocker. I want to be wise. Please tender my heart when someone is willing to make the effort to help me grow. Give me the wisdom to refrain from rebuking those who will only be angry and reject it.

Wiser Still

Instruct the wise and they will be wiser still;
teach the righteous and they will add to their learning.
PROVERBS 9:9 NIV

Why does a wise person love rebuke? They know it will help them become even wiser. A teachable person cares more about the truth than their fragile image. Their pride does not block their view, for their eyes are set on God. To be corrected and learn encourages a wise person. They turn to the Word of God to better themselves rather than justify their questionable behavior. Furthermore, a wise person is willing to change and readjust their lifestyle. They learn from those in positions over or under them because they know all wisdom comes from God, and God uses whomever he desires.

Instead of despising God's commands, a wise person embraces them gratefully because they understand they are guidelines to the best possible life. In Isaiah 5:20-21 the prophet warned, "Woe to those who call evil good and good evil, who put darkness for light and light for darkness, who put bitter for sweet and sweet for bitter. A wise person doesn't become confused like that because their compass is God and not themselves.

Teach me your righteousness, Lord God, and instruct me to be wise.

Beginning of Wisdom

The fear of the Lord is the beginning of wisdom,
and knowledge of the Holy One is understanding.
Proverbs 9:10 NIV

Hopefully you understand that *fear* in this verse is not a feeling of terror but of awe. It's a dawning of understanding and an awakening of truth. Submission to God is where we finally start to get a grip on our position in life and the reality of our existence. For most of us, this is not a momentous event. The verse says this awe is the beginning of something: our path with God. The rest of the journey is more manageable if we understand why we experience what we do.

We aren't much of a testimony when we're healthy, happy, and rich. People attribute our lives to ease and comfort, which does not give a person compassion or empathy. Our struggles and difficulties are where we live out our faith in, and our fear of, God. That's when people will notice our Creator carries us to the other side of these rough spots.

Lord God Almighty, may you lift my eyes to you when I struggle in my life. Please give me understanding so I know why I'm here and why I depend on you. I am in awe of you.

Blessings of Faith

"By me your days will be multiplied,
And years of life will be added to you."
PROVERBS 9:11 NKJV

A life of faith is a life that will be prolonged so its testimony can spread. Trusting God to number our days has widespread consequences. That depth of trust can result in a longer life. God loves willing workers and able hands as his disciples. He wants us to be part of his plan to spread the good news to all the world. Living a life of wisdom means relying on God to define the meaning of life. That's a deep dependency, but nothing less is sufficient for our Maker. He is worthy, and he alone is able.

A highlight of a believer's life is that this life is temporary. A long life might just be a healthy set of genetics, or it might be a call to keep working for the kingdom. Whatever length of life we are given doesn't matter in the end because we will live eternally with our Father in heaven. What does matter is how we serve God before we are called home. These days matter only for the purpose of taking everyone you can reach with you into eternity.

Dear God, bless my works and words so I may reach everyone and anyone you have put in my life. May I be a vessel for you.

Consequences

If you become wise, you will be the one to benefit.
If you scorn wisdom, you will be the one to suffer.
PROVERBS 9:12 NLT

Most often, a stable life can result from making good decisions, and poor choices will likely lead to more drama and upheaval. This isn't always the case, but it certainly seems to be Solomon's advice and God's wisdom for God's people. Blessings abound for those who have eyes to see, and we can't see clearly without God's truth thriving in our hearts.

On the other hand, turning away from the truth found in God's Word has dire consequences. We are warned constantly that scorning God and his wisdom will lead to a trip down a rough road. This will be true for those who turn away from God as well as their families and loved ones. Grief and pain are everywhere. May we always, without judgment, reach out with wisdom as a soothing balm to draw those suffering into the love and eternal peace of God's kingdom.

Dear Father, give me wisdom. Please open my heart to your truth and grant me grace to live according to your Word.

Unwise Noise

Foolishness is like a loud woman;
she does not have wisdom or knowledge.
PROVERBS 9:13 NCV

Here is the dichotomy between a loud fool and a quiet servant of the Lord. The loud woman who is a fool doesn't have wisdom or knowledge. The quiet person seeking God will praise him and be defended by in. In Psalm 46:10-11, God says, "'Be still and know that I am God. I will be praised in all the nations; I will be praised throughout the earth.' The Lord All-Powerful is with us; the God of Jacob is our defender." We are under God's protection, and as we seek him, we will be wise. As we search for his wisdom and knowledge, we will avoid being fools.

Not every loud woman is necessarily a fool; it says foolishness is *like* a loud woman. Someone who speaks without thinking, raising their voice above everyone else's, is foolish. A person of wisdom thinks before they speak and knows when to raise their voice.

Dear God, please direct my mouth. Teach me how to be still before you and not be loud. Teach me when to use my voice to be a good representative of you.

No Indulgence Refreshes

"Come in with me," she urges the simple.
To those who lack good judgment, she says,
"Stolen water is refreshing;
food eaten in secret tastes the best!"
PROVERBS 9:16-17 NLT

Countless adages tell us pleasure in the moment is often not worth the long-term results of a poor decision. Thankfully, the Bible doesn't just tell us to avoid being fools; it also defines foolishness. Today's verse is about self-indulgence. The voices of today tell us to go for gold or live our best life. A person can easily be distracted by the shiny carrot dangling on the path of cultural norms.

Knowing what the Word of God says is the first step. The eighth commandment tells us not to steal, so when the Foolish Woman in today's verse tells us that stolen water is good, that's a red flag. If we have to hide to eat our ill-gotten gains, maybe we shouldn't be eating it. Know God; believe his Word. Behave worthy of the kingdom because it's coming.

Lord my God, I love you with my whole heart. I want to know you and live for you. I need more of you so the indulgences in my life will lose their importance to me.

Wise Children

Wise children make their father happy,
but foolish children make their mother sad.
PROVERBS 10:1 NCV

We were once children who caused our parents grief. So many proverbs warn us about parenting. Our sin will crop up in our children's behavior, but the warnings we heed will have blessings. Proverbs offers a path through the turbulence of child-rearing to avoid the pain and grief of wayward offspring.

The only way to nurture wise children is to, purposefully and diligently, teach and train them the right qualities while staying close to the Lord. The only way to be wise as parents is to emulate the Lord in our words, actions, and attitudes. May we carefully keep these words of wisdom close to our hearts.

Dear Father, may I reflect you in the words, actions, and attitudes I present to the children in my life.

Right Living

Riches gotten by doing wrong have no value,
but right living will save you from death.
PROVERBS 10:2 NCV

Solomon said many wise things, but a famous topic he addresses is the pursuit of money. Proverbs 21:6 says, "Wealth that comes from telling lies vanishes like a mist and leads to death." As one of the wealthiest men to ever live and the recipient of wisdom from God, Solomon is the one to listen to. Not only is focusing on wealth a waste of time, it's also deadly.

On the other hand, if believers aspire to live righteously, we will avoid the distractions that will kill us. If we live in a relationship close to God and loving toward people, we will figure out the way of wisdom which leads to everlasting life.

Oh Lord, keep me close and attend to my heart. Let me see the path you have planned for me and show me wisdom in what I pursue.

The Righteous Eat

The Lord does not let the righteous go hungry,
but he thwarts the craving of the wicked.
Proverbs 10:3 ESV

It would be simplistic and silly to take this verse as judgment on any confessing Christian going hungry. God does not only see the temporal life. More important to him is the eternal life. We are eternal beings, and we will spend forever in heaven or hell. That is clear. So the righteous—those who seek and serve him throughout their lives—will eat the food of righteousness in heaven, and those who seek the path of selfishness and evil will be eternally thwarted in their desires.

Don't let the evil one fool you into thinking that the here and now is all we have. More important and pressing is the condition of our hearts which will determine the address of our eternal homes. Ultimately, now matters little when compared to then.

Dear Lord, keep my eyes on you and your eternal plan. May my heart not judge when I witness believers suffering; you know their eternal path. I pray my path leads straight to you.

Making Rich

Poor is one who works with a lazy hand,
But the hand of the diligent makes rich.
PROVERBS 10:4 NASB

If we work hard, we will do better than if we indulge in laziness. That is a life truth we can trust. It doesn't mean poverty necessarily points back to a lazy person; there are many reasons the Lord allows challenging finances in a person's life. It isn't something we can judge.

If you do see poverty resulting from laziness, it isn't surprising. Consequences are a powerful teacher, and the Lord uses them to move his people into deeper understanding and grace. We are told that to not work is a statement of the heart. We read in 1 Timothy 5:8 that "if anyone does not provide for his one, and especially for those of his household, he has denied the faith and is worse than an unbeliever." Keep going; be diligent; work hard. The consequences will be revealed over time.

Father God, keep me going. Please encourage me in the work I do and let me see your path so I will be uplifted in your purpose for me.

Gather in Summer

He who gathers in summer is prudent son,
but he who sleeps in harvest is a son who brings shame.
PROVERBS 10:5 ESV

We are not being kind to our children when we allow them to indulge in sinful tendencies. The Bible is clear that self-indulgence leads to death. Parents know the frustration of a lazy child who refuses to work when they are needed. Tough actions are called for in such circumstances. Parents offer up excuses in ill-conceived protection of their child's laziness, but nothing will undo the accompanying attitudes once these children have grown.

The life of a good parent doesn't mean they never extend grace to a tired or sick child. It means they see through the repetitive behavior that will hasten their child toward eternal death. Good representation of biblical behavior is a start, but it must also be accompanied by the expectation of a godly child.

Dear God, allow me to see through a child's behavior with godly vision. Let me discern with wisdom the actions needed to open heaven's doors to my offspring.

Receive Commandments

The wise of heart will receive commandments,
but a babbling fool will come to ruin.
PROVERBS 10:8 ESV

The blessing of Scripture, and Proverbs in particular, is we are told what a person whose heart is truly given over to God looks like. A lover of God will show certain signs, display certain characteristics, and have an attitude reflecting the Master. Fruit, borne by the Holy Spirit, will show up in God's people. John 13:35 says outsiders will know we are Christians by our love one for another.

The heart of a believer is fertile soil. We are softened by the Word of God working in us as living water. It changes us from the inside out and allows us to be teachable, open, and changeable. We will listen to the leading of the Holy Spirit. The path of life for an unbeliever will end in ruin because all that comes to a believer through the Spirit is missing.

Holy Spirit, gentle my heart and open my eyes to the truth you reveal. Let me be teachable and willing to become the person you intend me to be.

Walking Securely

Whoever walks in integrity walks securely,
but he who makes his ways crooked will be found out.
PROVERBS 10:9 ESV

Do you have secrets you think nobody notices? Our true natures are exposed when we think nobody is watching, but the effects are obvious whether we believe it or not. The value of a clear conscience can't be overstated. When your conscience is clean, your sleep is more peaceful, your mind less busy, your steps more secure, and your heart carries less fear and worry.

You never need to worry about being *found out* because there is nothing to hide. You can't be blackmailed, and your enemies have nothing to leverage against you. Any rumors or gossip formed at your expense will be proven wrong because your character will speak for itself. Dirty, little secrets are not worth the trouble. Besides, God always sees, and he cares too much about you to let your harm yourself like that. Anything hidden will be found out. It is better and simpler to live honorably and purely in public and in secret. Keep your conscience clear and get a good night's sleep.

Lord, I surrender everything in my life to you today. Thank you for giving me your strength to overcome.

Winking and Chattering

Whoever winks maliciously causes grief,
and a chattering fool comes to ruin.
PROVERBS 10:10 NIV

The behavior of a child of God is unique, and we don't start out with the ways of a new believer. Some changes are gradual, and some changes can be life-altering and sudden. Malicious behavior is self-serving and based in humoring or entertaining without concern for the feelings of the victim. A person can consider themselves funny or popular because they are willing to use someone as fodder for their jokes and pokes.

Additionally, if a person speaks incessantly with the intention of just filling the air with wrongly perceived wisdom or wit, they delude themselves. Instead of idle chatter, a Christian should consider their words and speak only with concern and kindness for others. The path of a believer leads to eternal life, and an unbeliever will end in ruin. Choose carefully.

Father, close the door to my pre-Christian life and all the broken behaviors that came with that life. Please guide my tongue and my outlook toward you and all that edifies you.

Fountain of Life

The mouth of the righteous is a fountain of life,
but the mouth of the wicked conceals violence.
PROVERBS 10:11 ESV

The book of James is only five chapters, but it is full of good direction for behavior. It is famous for the "faith without works is dead" sermon but also for the descriptions of the power of the tongue. Chapter 3 describes how the tongue is a fire and can set a whole forest ablaze. It compares the tongue to a bit in a horse's mouth and how the whole horse is steered by this little metal device. James also talks about the relatively small rudder of a ship which moves the massive vessel with little movements.

Don't downplay the impact of your words. Today's verse was written almost a thousand years before the book of James was written. God has always warned his followers to use their speech carefully because it will reflect the true condition of the heart and either spread the good news about eternity or hurt others.

Lord my God, be the director of my soul and the ruler of my heart so I can reflect your love with my tongue. May I speak life to all who are near me.

Love Versus Hate

Hatred stirs up strife,
But love covers all offenses.
PROVERBS 10:12 NASB

A plethora of relationship tips and advice can ease the sting of strife, but nothing can replace the tough labor of love. Only love can heal wounds instead of covering them up. Only love can counteract and overcome hate. Offenses may grow deeper or dimmer in time, but only love can put them to rest. Hatred and apathy destroy and tear down, but love fixes and builds up.

Within each of us is the potential for love or hate: for building up or breaking down. When we are offended, our sinful nature wants to get even and make the other person experience the same hurt we experienced, but that's not how godly love works. We have been forgiven of much, and we have the amazing opportunity to now forgive others. Extending forgiveness is one way of showing God how grateful we are for the undeserved forgiveness he showed us. Let's retaliate against hatred with love and watch the world change before our eyes.

Help me not succumb to offense, dear Lord, and give me the courage to respond with love.

Back and Rod

Wisdom is found on the lips of him who has understanding,
But a rod is for the back of him who is devoid of understanding.
PROVERBS 10:13 NKJV

God applies the rod to awaken understanding. That is a shocking statement in today's world, but we should not be shocked. Whether it's a physical rod or another punishment, we should be shocked that so many people are willing to bypass disciplining their children, so they grow up with disobedience in their hearts. These attitudes will lead our children into eternal punishment.

Understanding is a result of discipline. If you had parents who disciplined, praise God for them. If not, you have a more difficult road to learn how to discipline your children. But God has overcome much greater difficulties, and he will lead you in this challenge. Love is not missing in discipline. A greater love can't be found than the love that leads to eternity in heaven.

Lord God, teach me how to discipline effectively and righteously. Give me eternal eyes so I can discern right from wrong.

May
Commit to the Lord
whatever you do,
and he will establish your plans.
Proverbs 16:3 NIV

Don't Tell All

The wise don't tell everything they know,
but the foolish talk too much and are ruined.
PROVERBS 10:14 NCV

A common phrase today is, "It's better to be thought a fool than to open your mouth and prove it." It's a spin on today's verse, although what people think about you isn't the most important point. It's more important to consider what God thinks about you. Seeking and knowing God results in wisdom, and you learn from him how to be quiet and when to speak. When you do speak, you will know what to say.

Ignoring God or walking past opportunities to learn more about him will result in foolishness. Not knowing your Maker results in speech that will be the evidence of ignorance. You can rarely fool people when your behavior reflects your heart, and you can never fool God.

Dear God, please teach me. Keep me close to you so I learn how to emulate you in my speech and actions.

The Strong City

The wealth of the rich is their fortress;
the poverty of the poor is their destruction.
PROVERBS 10:15 NLT

Neither of the options in today's verse is ideal. If a person's wealth offers them protection from the storms in life, they will have little tendency to seek the Lord. Likewise, if a person is so poor that they succumb to stealing and other immoral behaviors, they walk away from their divine protector and provider. Both wealth and poverty offer untenable situations that pull a person away from a healthy relationship with the Creator.

Dear believer, pray for a balanced life. Pray for enough but never too much. Pray for bills to be paid and food on the table rather than fancy houses or vehicles. If we have a gross excess above our daily bread, housing, and transportation, we can become dependent on our stuff rather than on God. Matthew 6:33 tells us to "Seek the Kingdom of God above all else, and righteously, and he will give you everything you need."

Dear God, may I have enough but not too much. May I have work that provides for my family. Make me content to trust you to take care of the future.

Wages of Righteousness

The wages of the righteous is life,
but the earnings of the wicked are sin and death.
PROVERBS 10:16 NIV

The concept of work is infused throughout the Bible right from God's work in the creation of the world in Genesis 2:2 through to Revelation where God draws attention to both good work as well as the work of the evil one. Make no mistake, the good work has its wages, and so does the work of the wicked.

We are blessed to know exactly what is expected of the follower of God. Do not stagnate in your relationship with your God; he wants you to follow him and continually seek his wisdom. He will reveal the unfolding pages of your life in the best possible choices. You will have the nod of approval from your Maker when you are one of the righteous ones. If you turn away from God, however, the sin you have not repented of will lead to eternal death.

Lead me, oh God, down your path of righteousness. Keep me knowledgeable to your ways so I clearly see the difference between good and evil.

Correction and Discipline

Whoever heeds discipline shows the way to life,
but whoever ignores correction leads others astray.
PROVERBS 10:17 NIV

Living contrary to Gods instruction hurts not only us but those closest to us as well. Our family and friends will be negatively impacted or even led astray if we ignore God's correction. Remember, God corrects and disciplines us because he loves us and wants the best for us. Accepting discipline and correcting our ways will increase our spiritual maturity, and that becomes a blessing to us and others in our lives.

Since we are in the body of Christ, we grow together, hurt together, and mature together. None of us are individually impacted because that's not how a body works. It's important for us to heed discipline so we can show others the way to life. Being able to share our faith and be a blessing to others is an incredible gift; let's not waste it.

Lord, when you correct me, please give me the wisdom to respond maturely. You discipline me because you love me.
I can grow, learn, and teach others also.

Hatred and Slander

Whoever hides hatred has lying lips,
And whoever spreads slander is a fool.
PROVERBS 10:18 NKJV

The condition of the heart is a big deal to God. He needs complete honesty for confessions of sin and repentance for it. 1 John 3:15 says, "Whoever hates his brother is a murderer, and you know that no murderer has eternal life abiding in him." Solomon was also aware of the severe consequences of keeping hatred in your heart while professing otherwise with your mouth. If you are secretly resenting someone, come clean and confess it to God. He will walk you through the process of honest repentance.

On the other hand, some people make no effort to hide the condition of their hearts. These people slander and defame others without hesitation, and they are simply fools. Ultimately, Proverbs spells out the consequence of being a fool, and that is death. Fools spend eternity separated from God.

Father, reveal to me any secret hatred or animosity in my heart. Help me be completely honest with myself but mostly with you, oh Lord. May I depend upon you to forgive my sin for my eternal blessing.

Talk less

If you talk a lot, you are sure to sin;
if you are wise, you will keep quiet.
PROVERBS 10:19 NCV

We are told throughout Proverbs to be quiet. For those of us who are chatty, this is a challenge, but it's an important discipline to cultivate. The quieter we are, the more we will hear. The more we hear, the more we will know the griefs and challenges of people around us. The more we know our people, the more we can address the needs of their lives and souls.

As we listen to people, the act of being quiet will feed our growth in wisdom. How amazing that we can learn a few simple disciplines which then grow into big character developments. The first step in faith blooms blessings right under the feet of those following in the footsteps of Jesus.

Grow me, Lord, in your everlasting way. Take my tiny footsteps of faith and make me a pillar of strength in you.

Tongue of Silver

The tongue of the righteous is choice silver;
the heart of the wicked is of little worth.
PROVERBS 10:20 ESV

There are four precious metals: gold, silver, platinum, and palladium. They are considered precious because they either maintain a consistently high value, or they are in demand and relatively rare. Silver has unique qualities because it conducts electricity and heat best out of all the elements. It is also beautiful for making jewelry and antimicrobial for fighting bacteria. Isn't it fun that Solomon, not knowing all of this, compares the tongue of the righteous to this beautiful metal?

The righteous tongue speaks beautiful words that will fight the toxicity of sick words. We can't fake this; our words will reflect the condition of our hearts. They can be functional and beautiful like precious metal, silver, or they can be of little worth like the words of the unrighteous.

Lord, guide my tongue and teach me to give my heart to you so the outpouring of my mouth is as precious as silver.

Righteous Lips Feed

The lips of the righteous feed many,
but fools die for lack of sense.
PROVERBS 10:21 ESV

The food in the mouth of a righteous person is not necessarily just meat and potatoes. We also need food for the soul. This verse likely possesses, as many verses do in Scripture, a double meaning. As God's people, we feed many in soup kitchens and the homes of the sick and infirm. This act of love and service is an outpouring of our love for God. We need to feed the hungry; we also need to speak about the gospel.

It shouldn't surprise believers when we understand eternal life, and consequently the deeper aspects of this life as well, better than unbelievers do. We are infused with the Holy Spirit who is the director and teacher of truth. Christ promised to leave us his Spirit, and from him we know the truth. Rather than lofting us into a spiritual stratosphere, this awareness should humble us knowing we are unworthy of such a gift. Gratefulness propels us to spread this mystifying and beautiful truth.

Teach and train me, oh Spirit, to the truth about your presence in my life and the consequences of living as a believer in a fallen world.

Blessing without Sorrow

The blessing of the LORD makes rich,
and he adds no sorrow with it.
PROVERBS 10:22 ESV

The wealth of knowing God is eternal. The glimpses of our future home through our blessings now are beautiful and satisfying. The yearning in our hearts culminates in the wonders of heaven. This richness will add no sorrow to our lives. Money on this side of heaven, however, can know much sorrow. It is the reason Luke tells us we cannot serve both God and money. If we serve God, we will have an eye toward heaven. Money may happen, or it may not. That is for the Lord to decide. May we be good stewards of money, but may we always be grateful for our blessings no matter what form they take.

It is a blessing to not want for our earthly needs. It is also a blessing to not have too much wealth because it comes with much responsibility. It is a blessing to have good health, but the burdens of the sick can open doors to people, and the good news is often spread by the testimonies of those who suffer.

Father, thank you for my blessings. May I always be aware of the goodness that comes from you.

Delight in Wisdom

A fool finds pleasure in wicked schemes,
but a person of understanding delights in wisdom.
Proverbs 10:23 NIV

It can be either a strength or a weakness that we gravitate toward people like us. If we are in good standing with the Lord, that's great. If we are on a path of poor choices, there are reasons to be concerned. For anyone who remembers living as an unbeliever, this attraction to one set of behaviors over another has a clear dividing line. We reject the sinful nature we willingly entertained before being saved. We are born again and are grateful to be people of understanding who delight in wisdom.

Wicked schemes are fun and entertaining for those who don't follow God. When we see this behavior, it defines the condition of that person's heart. Rather than condemning the person, let's pray for their heart. Let's show God's love and grace and reflect his love, grace, and renewal.

Father, thank you. Thank you for showing me the light and saving me from the dark. Thank you for making me a person of understanding and teaching me how to show grace to others.

Dreads and Desires

What the wicked dreads will come upon him,
but the desire of the righteous will be granted.
PROVERBS 10:24 ESV

It's scary to imagine suffering from the very thing you dread. How horrifying! Standing on the Word of God means taking these statements of Solomon's seriously. Although Solomon does speak from an eternal perspective, many of his proverbs are seen in this lifetime as well, but we can't downplay an eternity separated from God. That motivates the work we do for God. May we reach everyone we can through our words and actions. May our lives give testimony to the wonder of an eternity with God.

There is beauty in the pure desires of a believer. As we grow closer to God, our desires become his desires. Our selfishness fades, and our awareness of others increases. We become part of the body of Christ as his beloved church.

Make and mold me into the likeness of you, oh God. Allow my desires to become like yours.

Wicked Gone

When the storm has swept by, the wicked are gone,
but the righteous stand firm forever.
PROVERBS 10:25 NIV

Although we don't know when they will occur, the end times are inevitable. We are told to watch for the signs, and every generation does. We look to climactic changes, political upheavals, and family disunity, and we know the times are coming. There could be a lot of fear, knowing the truth and understanding the inevitable, but we are instructed in the Word not to fear. If we understand the deeper stream of truth under the disintegration of our earthly lives, we know we are destined for an amazing life in eternity.

We stand firm because we are told to do so. We trust God because we know he is worthy. We keep our eyes firmly pointed toward heaven because we will sink into despair if we don't. What is coming is one of the greatest displays of our omniscient Father in all of history. May all the glory be God's!

Dear Jesus, please still my heart and keep me pointed toward you. Let me see you in the events around me so I know your plan is firmly in place.

Vinegar and Smoke

Like vinegar to the teeth and smoke to the eyes,
so is the sluggard to those who send him.
PROVERBS 10:26 ESV

Even in biblical times, people knew vinegar could eat away at teeth. We now know more about the science behind the process: vinegar can erode the outer layer of the enamel and bring tooth decay and cavities. Like so many things that are bad for you, however, vinegar can also be good for the teeth. If vinegar is used in reduced quantities or diluted, it can help whiten and strengthen teeth. Smoke is unreservedly bad for the eyes, but it also repels mosquitoes and can preserve delicious salmon and other meats.

Christians are led to a life of balance and a tension between good and evil. That doesn't mean our behavior can waffle between both sides of the fence. While our bodies exist in a sinful state this side of eternity, our souls yearn for purity and the presence of God. May we also yearn to bring as many people as possible with us into the kingdom.

Dear Lord Almighty, please give me discerning eyes and a yearning heart for righteousness and purity. May I be aware of the tension between good and evil yet purposeful in my walk toward you.

Fear of the Lord

The fear of the Lord *prolongs life,*
but the years of the wicked will be short.
Proverbs 10:27 ESV

Our souls long to worship. People who worship the Creator have found the only one who is worthy. Once that relationship with God is established, the pieces of our lives fall into place. Life will still have hills and valleys, but it's purposeful; it makes sense spiritually.

Self-focus distracts from our godly focus. When people overthink their wants and needs, they spiral into spending time with their emotions and indulgences. When a believer starts to focus on God and others, they are blessed with comforts and blessings they didn't even know they wanted. The satisfaction in a life spent with the Lord can't be underestimated because he is our fortress and fulfillment. We can't fully understand until we honestly and truly give ourselves to God. May our fear in him be everlasting and motivational.

Father, thank you. I am grateful to have you, your Word, and the invitation to communicate with you through prayers and observations of your creation. You are awesome and wonderful.

Eternal Hope

The hope of the righteous brings joy,
but the expectation of the wicked will perish.
PROVERBS 10:28 ESV

Hope for the future in this life is not the hope that today's verse is referring to. Hope is eternal; this life has death. We already know there will be both joy and tragedy in this lifetime, but the ultimate story remains the same for each of us. We get one life, and its terminus is sometime before a hundred and twenty years. For a believer, that is where hope begins. We do not hope for now; we hope for eternity.

Believers live now as if they will live forever. Our pure hearts and everlasting aspirations lead to our eternal lives. We do not have the expectations unbelievers have. We do not ask for wealth and comfort now although those are blessings when we have them. We seek God's face because true hope is found there.

My Lord and my God, I am in awe of what you have given me since I started to follow you. Please grow me even more as I learn to love as you love and live as you live.

Refuge and Ruin

The way of the LORD is a refuge for the blameless,
but it is the ruin of those who do evil.
PROVERBS 10:29 NIV

Maybe the ruin of those who do evil is the beginning of their lives with God. Believers hope for the salvation of every single person just as God desires no one should perish. That hope drives us to pray for our loved ones and our local and global community. We are alert to the degradation of our society and of so many cultures before us. We live in fallen world, and that is not lost on those who know the Word.

Our refuge is our Lord. As we read in today's verse, the way of the Lord is our refuge. The way of the Lord and the way of man are contrasted throughout Proverbs. We have a choice between the two. If we are not taking the way of the Lord, which is a narrow and specific direction, then we are taking the way of man which leads to death. It is wise to seek the Lord and know his way.

Take each of my steps, oh Lord, and put them on your path. May my eyes be opened by your Word which is a lamp to my feet.

The Righteous Stay

The righteous will never be removed,
but the wicked will not dwell in the land.
PROVERBS 10:30 ESV

There is only one way to be righteous: to submit our lives to God. We are assured that our place in the land is solid but only if we are righteous. Submission to God is not a one-and-done decision. It is an active, constant state of mind. At any moment, our hearts and minds can wander into sin because that is the human condition. However, the righteous actively seek their Lord in those moments and bring their hearts back into a kingdom focus.

The discipline necessary to repent of sin whenever it crops up pulls us into the best life with God. We can't understand his ways fully without consistent and constant repentance. That submission will open our eyes and hearts to the character and personality of our Father.

Oh God, bend my heart toward you. Teach me your ways. Thank you for the assurance that you will protect us and keep us near you.

Fruit of Wisdom

From the mouth of the righteous comes the fruit of wisdom,
but a perverse tongue will be silenced.

PROVERBS 10:31 NIV

As we learn the Word of God, we start to enjoy the intellect and beauty of our perfect Maker. God is bigger than us in every way. When we enjoy learning something new, exploring a puzzle, or reading a challenging book, that's because we serve a smart god. He is love and so much more. He is compassion, and he touches the depths of our core needs. We desire to learn, explore, and share with others because our Lord is also excited by these things.

Once we start down the path to eternity, what we speak about and share with others will reflect the character of God. We will tap into his wisdom and excitement for learning and sharing. God assures us that his righteous people will speak. We will have a voice that reflects him, and those opposed to him will finally be quiet.

May I speak as one who is righteous, oh Father. May I edify you in everything I say, and may your people be lifted up in the perfection of your Word.

What Is Acceptable

The lips of the righteous know what is acceptable,
but the mouth of the wicked, what is perverse.
PROVERBS 10:32 ESV

When the Word is in our hearts, the right words will come out of our mouths. When we do not have the Word in our lives, the sinful nature we are all born with comes out of our mouths. Paul says in Romans that we first believe in our hearts, but it is when we confess with our mouths that we are saved. God takes very seriously what comes out of our mouths.

It is acceptable to praise God. It is acceptable to edify and lift each other up. It is acceptable to speak the truth in kindness and love. May the Lord convict each of us about what is not acceptable. May we know what God considers perverse because culture and sin will taint the truth. The Word of God will plant seeds of righteousness in our hearts, and the Holy Spirit will guide and teach us as we seek to know our Father.

Lead me, God, to know your ways. Teach me about what is acceptable and what is perverse. Please seal my lips when I am tempted to say anything that does not edify you.

Accurate Weights

The Lord detests the use of dishonest scales,
but he delights in accurate weights.
Proverbs 11:1 NLT

Deception is a heart issue. It does matter, of course, if the numbers on the tax return are almost where they should be or the hours on the timecard include the time on social media. But what matters more is the evil going to work in the heart when these deceptions are being considered.

God loves it when goodness goes to work in the heart. When we accurately record the numbers, we honor God. When we are generous with the babysitter's pay and the attention paid to the children after a long day at work, the Holy Spirit is joyful. These little decisions for righteousness grow us in minuscule steps that may not amount to much in the moment, but they are a battle won for the kingdom.

Father God, forgive me for my deceptions. I want to serve you, in the tiniest details of my life. I want your Spirit to be at work in every part of my existence.

Avoid the Ego

When pride comes, then comes disgrace,
but with humility comes wisdom.
PROVERBS 11:2 NIV

Every time we open our mouths, may it be in humility rather than pride. May the words we speak be edifying to God and uplifting to each other. Instead of stroking our egos and showing off our knowledge, let's listen to what others have to say and allow God to lift us up in his time and his way. Pride is detrimental to our faith and only leads to disgrace, but the words of the wise are humble, loving, patient, and praiseworthy.

Let's be people others can feel comfortable and safe around. Let's not get caught in trying to prove ourselves or compare with others. Instead, the endeavor of our lives ought to be to point others back to Christ. He is where all good things flow from. All we are and all we have are gifts from him. Let's use our gifts to be a blessing to others.

I want to praise you in everything, dear Jesus. I don't want to become trapped in the ego game of trying to measure up against others. I know you love me the way I am, and you created me to bring you praise.

Integrity of the Upright

The integrity of the upright guides them,
but the crookedness of the treacherous destroys them.
PROVERBS 11:3 ESV

Integrity is hard won. It takes work and persistence. The irony about shortcuts is they are not really time-savers at all; they work against us. Even worse, they work against eternity with God. When God's righteousness is infused in his people, more people see and appreciate that lifestyle, and more souls are won for God.

Integrity breeds itself, and so does crookedness. Once a decision has been made, the following decisions repeat the pattern. Crookedness takes little effort; it only requires self-indulgence. Integrity, however, requires introspection, consideration, and selflessness. A purposeful life is a rich life, but a person doesn't learn that without engaging the more challenging characteristics first.

Lord, guide me so I learn what it means to be truly infused with your goodness and integrity. Allow me to take on your insight, personality, and vision.

Righteousness Delivers

Wealth is worthless in the day of wrath,
but righteousness delivers from death.
PROVERBS 11:4 NIV

At the end of days, *the day of wrath*, we will see the results of our earthly pursuits. The real meaning of life will play out before us in the ultimate judgment of what we gave weight to while we went about our daily lives. Eternity isn't trivial or distant. What we do now has weight whether we acknowledge it or not, and it's better to acknowledge it.

That acknowledgement, although weighty, doesn't have to be a burden. The burden isn't ours. We are to seek first the kingdom of God and his righteousness. After that, everything we need and much of what we desire will be given to us. Check out Matthew 6:33. Eyes up and then, amazingly, the shackles of this life will loosen. As we gaze toward heaven, we will be living eternally instead of temporally, and the difference gives us wings.

Lord, my God, sustain me. Although I am bound by this body now, give me wings. Allow me to be grateful for every breath here on earth, but please also give the glimpses of eternity so I can see my purpose.

The Smooth Way

The righteousness of the blameless will smooth his way,
But the wicked will fall by his own wickedness.
PROVERBS 11:5 NASB

Tripping is a hazard in life, and in some seasons, like babyhood and old age, it's more frequent. Tripping is a physical reminder of a spiritual reality. When we trip spiritually, it points to the fact that we aren't paying enough attention to important aspects of being a believer.

An example of spiritual tripping is a slip of the tongue. Maybe an accidental curse word pops out, or we say a rude comment to a coworker or family member. It can be shocking to both parties. Maybe plans leave a person too worn out to go to church. Perhaps daily time with God is not a priority, and it's been a few days, a week, or more. Pay attention! The road is smooth and obvious when we are with our Lord; we are spiritually alive and sparkling with conversations with him. The bumpy road leads to stumbling and falling away from God.

Keep my eyes on you, God. Keep my focus where it will edify you.

The Right Rescue

The godliness of good people rescues them;
the ambition of treacherous people traps them.
PROVERBS 11:6 NLT

If we understand that the God who created us knows what's best, then we understand why he defined a healthy standard of behavior. God's requirement for his followers is clear: behave as he would. God sent his Son who lived that standard perfectly. There is no question about what he wants us to do and how he wants us to live. He walked this planet. He knows.

When God tells us through Solomon that we will be rescued when we are godly, we know the behavior that emulates his behavior will steer us away from eternal disaster. When God tells us that treacherous people can't have healthy ambitions and their plans will trap them in untenable situations, our souls can rejoice that we serve the living God.

Dear Jesus, teach me to live as you lived and base my decisions on the very heart of the Father.

Hope That Dies

When the wicked die, hope dies with them;
their hope in riches will come to nothing.
PROVERBS 11:7 NCV

We each get one lifetime to figure out the purpose of life, and we can enjoy the blessings both now and forever if we figure it out earlier rather than later. The resounding peace within the soul that comes with an active relationship with the Creator can't be understated. The knowledge of an everlasting life, of which earthly life is only a small fraction, catapults every thought and motive in a way nothing else can.

Contrast that with the discontent and limited vision of a person who lives only for their earthly selves. The mind of such a person spins in on itself and not into time immemorial. A lack of eternal motivation leaves only self, and self is never satisfying nor satisfied. To never know the love of God is unfathomably sad. Knowing his love? Unfathomably glorious.

Dear Father, thank you for choosing me to follow you into eternity. My heart, mind, and soul have been changed forever to feel and think in a way an unbeliever never can. Please bring salvation to those unbelievers.

Trouble Visits

The righteous is delivered from trouble,
And it comes to the wicked instead.
PROVERBS 11:8 NKJV

An old idiom says, "Don't trouble trouble till trouble troubles you." Perhaps it came from this proverb. If we don't engage problems, and if we have the insight and resources to bypass issues when they press into our lives, we will save ourselves a lot of bother. This idiom, however, is only half baked.

The reverse of it is also true. When we invite trouble into our lives through bad decisions, compromised relationships, and questionable pastimes, there's a snowball effect of troubles just waiting to happen. That is what today's proverb tells us. Solomon knew this three thousand years ago, so we weren't left to figure this out on our own. Scripture tells us exactly what to expect.

Lord God, keep me holy in heart, mind, and soul. Allow me the insight to see when trouble is coming my way and deliver me from it.

Resourcefulness

With words an evil person can destroy a neighbor,
but a good person will escape by being resourceful.
PROVERBS 11:9 NCV

Sometimes the best answer in a conflict is to say nothing at all. Scripture tells us to love our neighbor, and that is both literal and figurative. A person doesn't share living space with a neighbor, but we do share property lines, noise levels, and cooking smells. It's a close relationship. There will be conflicts, and today's verse tells us how to manage those difficulties.

The art of being resourceful covers a multitude of options. One option is to smile and keep walking. It may take ages to relax that neighbor, but the lack of conflict will help. Sometimes it's important to engage the neighbor in an uplifting way; for example, taking overbaked goods or having a simple visit. Sometimes it means doing extra yard work that ignores property lines. In every case, it requires the believer to suppress self-righteousness in favor of eternal outreach.

Lord, humble me and use me for your beautiful purposes. Allow me to be your vessel regardless of my feelings and teach me to manage my face and feelings so your glory can show through.

A City Rejoices

When it goes well with the righteous, the city rejoices,
and when the wicked perish there are shouts of gladness.
PROVERBS 11:10 ESV

The Creator impressed on each of us a sense of righteousness. Even those who deny God adhere to a measure of right and wrong. If the Holy Spirit does not dwell in a person, that measure is based only on self and is selfish. During our earthly lives, our communities are also skewed in the measure of righteousness. The celebration of good things happening to a community's citizenry can be, but is not usually, based on God's created order.

When a believer's citizenship is founded in heaven, however, all of heaven rejoices every time a good thing happens to one of its people, and that is based on pure righteousness. We have an eternal place where we belong, and our welfare is important to each person in that place.

Lord, keep me near you so I can understand the depth of my belonging. Allow me to know you as well as your people both now and in heaven.

Build the City

Good people bless and build up their city,
but the wicked can destroy it with their words.
PROVERBS 11:11 NCV

The heart of a believer is infused with the will of God. We bless and do not harm. We build and do not break down. We love and do not hate. At least, that's the goal. None of us can perfectly keep that standard. We can, however, perfectly aspire to it because the Holy Spirit is in us, motivating us, checking our hearts, and welcoming our repentance. Diligent attendance to our relationships with the Almighty God will open doors to his will playing out in us.

This pure motivation is vacant in unbelievers. Even do-gooders are motivated by a selfish feeling or gain. Even the flush of acknowledgment when a community service is accomplished can be a motivator. Believers, avoid the sinful heart and keep a healthy check on motivations. Do good for the kingdom and not for your personal sense of goodness.

Lord, purify my heart. Teach me your ways so I may live according to your truth. Grant me a pure heart so I may honor you.

Nice to Neighbors

It is foolish to belittle one's neighbor;
a sensible person keeps quiet.
PROVERBS 11:12 NLT

It takes discipline to not speak when it's obvious you're right! But delusions of righteousness are not the same as God's righteousness, and God, through Solomon, says it's foolishness to belittle a neighbor. Conflict with those in our neighborhoods or workplaces is inevitable. Just because you share office space or a street doesn't mean you have anything else in common. What is common is a smorgasbord of beliefs, backgrounds, and traditions.

There lies the opportunity for spiritual growth and the means to forward the kingdom. If we are like-minded with neighbors and coworkers, then they are already in the kingdom, or we are too much like the world. Test this hypothesis and use it as an opportunity to check yourself. If we have an opportunity to emulate Christ by not belittling a neighbor, that's a win. If we exercise the discipline of being quiet and sensible, the kingdom rejoices.

Dear Lord Almighty, live in me, move through me, and rest in me. May I be Spirit-led in my words and behavior.

June

In their hearts
humans plan their course,
but the Lord *establishes*
their steps.

Proverbs 16:9 niv

Secrets

A gossip betrays a confidence,
but a trustworthy person keeps a secret.
PROVERBS 11:13 NIV

Are you a trustworthy person? Do other people know they are safe to share with you? Our integrity before God ought to matter more than our social standings. When someone confides in you, they are trusting you with a piece of themselves. Other people's secrets are never to be used to advance our reputations with others.

Trustworthy people keep the secrets of others safe. Gossip is deplorable before God because trust is hard to earn and easily broken. Let's be careful to love, care for, and protect others who have placed their trust and fragile secrets in our hands.

You are a safe place for me, God, and I want to be a safe place for others. When I am tempted to use someone's information for personal gain, remind me how precious trust is and help me keep my mouth shut. I want to be a trustworthy person who truly cares about others.

Don't Walk Alone

Where there is no guidance the people fall,
But in an abundance of counselors there is victory.
PROVERBS 11:14 NASB

God gives us each other to help us stay accountable, to encourage and motivate us so we can keep learning and growing, and so we never need to go through life alone. It is important we surround ourselves with people who love God and are willing to share their wisdom.

Attempting to go through life isolated, depending only on our personal strength, is foolish and prideful. We were not created to be cut off from others. The best way to ensure our victory is by working together and leaning on each other. Community and fellowship are two of God's great gifts.

Wonderful Counselor, when the day feels heavy, remind me to ask for help. Sometimes I don't want to burden others with my problems, but then I remember we are one body and one family under you, and we want the same thing. I want to worship you with my life.

Cautious Pledges

*Whoever puts up security for a stranger will surely suffer,
but whoever refuses to shake hands in pledge is safe.*
PROVERBS 11:15 NIV

Pledging was considered a legal contract by most people in biblical times. Numbers 30:2 says, "When a man makes a vow to the Lord or takes an oath to obligate himself by a pledge, he must not break his word but must do everything he said." Jesus also had something to say on this matter in Matthew 5:37, "All you need to say is simply 'Yes' or 'No'; anything beyond this comes from the evil one."

Solomon warned us not to engage in deep commitment to a stranger. It is better to refuse to make a pledge than to take on an obligation that can put a person into debt or duty beyond expectation even for a follower of God. We must keep our lives simple, keep our commitments focused on the God's convictions, and be obligated to no one.

Lord, help me discern between the commitments you have called me to make and those which will burden me unnecessarily and distract me from the path you have chosen for me.

Respect or Wealth

A kind woman gets respect,
but cruel men get only wealth.
Proverbs 11:16 NCV

From the perspective of ancient times, this was a true statement. A kind woman would be upheld in her community more than a wealthy man if he were cruel. That is a powerful truth when Solomon makes it; he is saying kindness trumps wealth, and he was perhaps the wealthiest man who ever lived.

Respect is worthy of everything, but wealth is only wealth. Money comes and money goes; it is not what makes a person respectable. On the other hand, true, intentional kindness builds people up. It's uplifting and important for a community to feel connected. As king, Solomon must have thought a lot about his own wealth and how the Israelites considered him.

Dear God, you have called us into community as brothers and sisters, and I pray I will be kind to each person in my community. May I put behavior above wealth.

Kindness Comes Home

Those who are kind benefit themselves,
but the cruel bring ruin on themselves.
PROVERBS 11:17 NIV

Most of us know this proverb at a personal level. We know both cruel and kind people. It is more than an academic lesson to consider what we are like to others. It's a simple step to move from how we think about the behavior of others to considering how others think about us. A bit of introspection is a good thing; self-absorption is sin.

The balance between accountability and too much inward focus is tenuous. It takes heartfelt focus on our Lord and Savior to live with kindness to others. People can sense if kindness is based in selfishness or in an honest concern for others. Time in the Word and on our knees in prayer moves us to real concern.

Dear Jesus, take me into your arms and keep me focused on living with your heartfelt concern for people. Let me be kindness itself for your glory.

Sow Righteousness

The wicked man does deceptive work,
But he who sows righteousness will have a sure reward.
PROVERBS 11:18 NKJV

Each moment of our lives is an opportunity to choose God. Jesus said, "For he who is not against us is on our side" in Mark 9:40. Throughout Scripture, there are people who sow righteousness for God, and there are all the others. Living for God is a purpose that requires thoughtfulness and diligence. The benefit of purposefully following the Lord's ways is we are assured of a reward.

The greatest of all griefs is to be separated from God; the greatest of all rewards is to spend eternity with God. There is no halfway point between the two. You are living for God, or you're not. Dear believer, God took you seriously when he created you; please take him seriously as you read his Word and consider your eternity.

Father, keep my path straight and my work edifying to you. I praise you for your clear words about righteousness and eternity.

Life or Death

Godly people find life;
evil people find death.
PROVERBS 11:19 NLT

We have spent time with people who don't acknowledge God. Those are often forlorn conversations because people with the Holy Spirit living within them have a sense of eternity missing in those who live for only the here and now. That phrase is even stated with pride and a disturbing sense of independence. However, independence is a misnomer because it's just a lack of acknowledging God.

People are governed by a person—the triune God—and not a principle. We desperately want to place ourselves into a sensible world with parameters and logic. If we don't acknowledge God, then the governing principles we adhere to are self-made and will fail. Everything other than worshiping the God who created each of us is destined to fail as stated in 1 John 2:17: "And this world is fading away, along with everything that people crave. But anyone who does what pleases God will live forever."

Dear Father God, teach my heart to crave only you. Allow me to learn throughout my life, how to be ever closer to you.

Innocent Hearts

The LORD hates those with evil hearts
but is pleased with those who are innocent.
PROVERBS 11:20 NCV

At our very hearts, God knows us. He understands our motivations, he knows what triggers us, and he knows our strengths and weaknesses. He understands as only a Maker could what we need to be fulfilled. Our only true satisfaction comes from the one who knew us from the beginning.

At no point does God abandon us. Throughout life, we are welcome in his presence. When we choose to walk away from our Lord, he grieves. He hates what we become when we turn away from the holy path. If we harbor arrogance, dissension, or wickedness in our hearts, we know God hates us. If we shed innocent blood, devise evil plans, give false witness, or rush to do what is wrong instead of what is right, God hates us. Scripture is bold in these statements because God also loves us. He leaves no question as to what is right or wrong so we will come to him.

Dear Lord, convict me of your righteousness and lead me in your way everlasting. Please forgive me for all the sins I have committed and convict me when I need to repent.

Generational Righteousness

Be assured, the evil person will not go unpunished,
But the descendants of the righteous will be rescued.
PROVERBS 11:21 NASB

When Christ died, his blood, agony, and sacrifice paid for our rescue. We are truly free. While those who do not repent will spend eternity separated from God, the repentant will be with him, gazing at a restored Garden of Eden where the river of life flows from the throne of God and the tree of life is beside it as described in Revelation 21:1-2.

Even better news: we will be rescued from a list of things we need never suffer again. We will have no more tears, no more pain, and no more sorrow. There will be no more separation from God because death will be gone and conquered forever. Our rescue, because we repent and follow the living God, is the sweetest reward because it means eternity with our heavenly Father.

Oh God, thank you for rescuing me and giving me a path to eternity with you where I will no longer know grief, pain, or separation from you.

Gold on a Pig

Like a gold ring in a pig's snout
is a beautiful woman without discretion.
PROVERBS 11:22 ESV

The image in this verse is intentionally shocking. No matter how beautiful someone is, if they can't control their mouth, they are quite piggish. On top of this unflattering image, pigs also have more meaning in a Jewish context.

Pigs are in the unclean animal category for Jews and should never be eaten nor their carcasses touched as noted in Deuteronomy 14:8. Matthew warns people to not throw pearls into the pigpen because they will trample them and then turn on the thrower. That conjures up some rich imagery, A person may be beautiful, but without a controlled tongue, they become the bane of their family and a burden to the community.

Lord, help me control what I say. Teach me to speak in ways edifying and beautiful to you. Let me learn your gentle ways, oh God.

Wish for Good

Those who do right only wish for good,
but the wicked can expect to be defeated by God's anger.
PROVERBS 11:23 NCV

God's anger is righteous. It's fierce; it's retributive. The Hebrew word *'ap* is used to describe both human and godly anger, and it refers to nostrils. People in biblical times thought the feeling of anger originated in the nose. The Hebrew word for God's anger is *anap* which means "to breathe hard." You can see God's flaring nostrils in this imagery!

According to Romans 5:9, "we have been made right with God by the blood of Christ's death." Christ's death on the cross will save the ones who do right and believe in him, but it will not save the wicked from the wrath of God. That anger is fearsome, horrible, and what we deserve. Christ is worthy to be praised because this is what we would face without him.

Lord, open my eyes to the people who are ready to be saved. Open my mouth to speak of your righteousness and beauty so one more person can enter heaven with a humble and grateful heart.

One Who Scatters

There is one who scatters, and yet increases all the more,
and there is one who withholds what is justly due,
and yet it results only in poverty.
PROVERBS 11:24 NASB

Tithing is a matter of the heart. Matthew 6:21 tells us, "for where your treasure is, there your heart will be also." Clinging to money is a heart issue. If we aren't giving freely to those who in need, God will hold us accountable. He tells us in Matthew 10:8, "Freely you received, freely give." Scattering our possessions, food, time, and other resources to others is unbelievably freeing. God knew what he was doing when he instructed us to do so.

The Lord is concerned for our eternal souls. Rich and poor are saved and unsaved; that is not the issue here. What matters is that we are rich in the Holy Spirit, and we withhold nothing from him. If we withhold anything from God, it will result in spiritual poverty, and that is costly for the soul.

Give me a soul that yearns for you, Lord, and a heart that gives to others. May I have an eternal perspective that releases me from a worldly need to protect and preserve myself. All I need is your protection and provision.

Grateful and Generous

The generous soul will be made rich,
And he who waters will also be watered himself.
PROVERBS 11:25 NKJV

When we give what we have, we acknowledge that we've been blessed enough to share with others. If we don't have much and still share, we acknowledge that we trust God to fulfill our needs. The most generous people are the most grateful. Realizing what God has given us and developing a spirit of gratefulness leads to generosity.

We want to share with others because we are thankful for what God has shared with us. What's more, when we give, more will be given back to us. We can't out-give God, and our heavenly Father promises to take care of us. This may become apparent in areas other than finance. Rest assured; he waters those who water others.

Lord God, develop in me an attitude of gratefulness, and give me opportunities to be generous with what you've entrusted to me.

Sell the Grain

People curse those who keep all the grain,
but they bless the one who is willing to sell it.
Proverbs 11:26 NCV

Hoarding wealth when it is there to sell is sinful. We are to share what we have when we have it, or we will face God's wrath. God intends for us to be his voice, arms, and legs to people who need to hear about the good news. One of the most effective ways of doing that is to help people when they need it. Reaching out, sharing what we have, spending time in relationships that honor and point to Jesus Christ: all this is the intention of the Holy Spirit as we walk through our days in deference to him.

We can't keep our stinginess a secret. We are all too similar to get away with effectively hiding things about ourselves. As time goes on, truth is revealed, and there wasn't much point in masking it anyway. Live boldly; live transparently; be generous to a degree that is unquestionably from the heart of the Holy Spirit.

My sweet Lord, you make me and hold me in the palm of your hand. May I be a sweet aroma to you in the way I live and give.

Seek Favor

Whoever diligently seeks good seeks favor,
but evil comes to him who searches for it.
PROVERBS 11:27 ESV

There are only two paths through life: seek good or search for evil. Both paths will lead us to whatever we are looking for. The trick is that motivation is rooted in our hearts, and the only one who can see our hearts perfectly is God. We can hide nothing from him even if we deny the truth to ourselves. We aren't always boldly telling ourselves the truth about our hearts, but through prayer and a close relationship with God, we see ourselves clearly. Paul reminds us in 1 Corinthians 13:12 that "now we see in a mirror dimly, but then face to face. Now I know in part; then I shall know fully, even as I have been fully known."

Hide nothing purposefully from God or yourself. Spend time with God asking him to reveal the truth about yourself and others. That puts you in a position of strength when you are asked about your reasons for following God.

Lord, tell me truly where I need to grow and how my strengths can be used for your kingdom. Increase your Holy Spirit in me, Lord, and decrease me.

A Green Leaf

Those who trust in riches will be ruined,
but a good person will be healthy like a green leaf.
PROVERBS 11:28 NCV

We make decisions based on where we have placed our trust. If we doubt God or question his existence or care, it becomes a simple misstep to move trust into our efforts and whatever we can build ourselves. Our earnings and efforts become our god. We place our trust in the big house, complete with security cameras and safety lights, our money purchased. We can put our trust in family or authority, but Psalm 118:9 says, "It is better to trust the Lord than to trust princes."

The Lord will lead us to the right steps if we trust him first. He will let us know which person to marry, which job to take, where to live, and whom to vote for. We can trust God, and through that complete surrender, we find our goodness and growth.

Lord, forgive me when I lack trust in you. Let me grow closer to you so I will flourish in my life for your glory.

Trouble to the Family

Whoever brings trouble to his family
will be left with nothing but the wind.
A fool will be a servant to the wise.
PROVERBS 11:29 NCV

Bad decisions compound on each other, and so do good decisions. God's guiding hand will steer us when we can't discern between the two. He has omniscience and omnipotence we do not. Giving God authority over your life will bring the blessing of wisdom, which will not only bless you, but also your family and those around you at work and play.

It's not popular to call people foolish, but God's Word points at certain behaviors which reveal fools. According to Ecclesiastes 10:2, "the heart of a fool" inclines to the left, which means they keep returning to foolish behavior. Isaiah 32:6 warns that "A fool says foolish things and in his mind he plans evil." Proverbs grossly says, "As a dog returns to its vomit, so fools repeat their folly." The behavior attracts itself and repeatedly spins in its own behavior. It's not a pleasant rut to be stuck in.

Lord, keep my heart wise. Allow me to discern foolish behavior in myself and show me how to correct and repent of such behavior.

Gain Souls

The fruit of the righteous is a tree of life,
And one who is wise gains souls.
PROVERBS 11:30 NASB

May we always be vessels for the Holy Spirit. May we provide a fount through which the living water will flow. Ephesians 2:10 tells us that "we are His workmanship, created in Christ Jesus for good works, which God prepared beforehand that we would walk in them." The fruit we bear when working for Jesus is a tree of life. May we be wise in the Spirit and willing to gain souls by telling God's story.

The only wisdom comes from God, and the only way we can know wisdom is to know God. We will bear the fruit of the tree of life by seeking his face and spending time with him. The only way to do that is to read the Word and pray to the living God. He is our righteousness and our all-in-all.

Lord, keep me on the narrow path so I may bear fruit that displays your righteousness in me.

Repaid on Earth

If the righteous is repaid on earth,
how much more the wicked and the sinner!
PROVERBS 11:31 ESV

If a believer is eternally minded, it changes their perspective so dramatically that others know they are different. They care more about souls than houses or cars. They love people more than possessions or politics. They seek life-altering attitudes rather than feel-good times or momentary pleasures. This can't be hidden; the Light of the world shines brightly everywhere the Holy Spirit dwells.

Believers are not looking for immediate consequences in this lifetime. It helps to collect a paycheck and have enough to maintain life and limb, but overall, God is all that matters. God blesses us now often far beyond our hopes and dreams. When we keep our expectations based in the Word of God, when he blesses us abundantly, it brings a rush of love and gratefulness that we serve such an amazing father.

Thank you, loving Father, for giving me so much now. I serve you openly and willingly in this lifetime. When I have an abundance, I am humbled and awed.

Love Discipline

To learn, you must love discipline;
it is stupid to hate correction.
PROVERBS 12:1 NLT

It's not a lot of fun to be disciplined, but the wise person sees the benefits and the alternative. Proverbs is packed with the benefits of having wisdom and accepting God's discipline, but they boil down to tempered behavior with discernment, sensibility, and clarity. The benefits are potentially eternal, and that is an asset to consider when weathering a correction.

The alternative to accepting discipline is not good news. In this translation, it is *stupid* to reject and dislike correction. It leaves no option for learning, growing, or living within the will of God. It closes spiritual doors rather than revealing spiritual development. Solomon emphasized God's people need to be open to periodic realignment and welcome closeness to our Father.

Lord my God, thank you for your correction when my behavior and attitude are not what they need to be. Please help me understand what is happening so I grow in you rather than reject your ways.

Be Good

The Lord *approves of those who are good,*
but he condemns those who plan wickedness.
Proverbs 12:2 NLT

Believers can get into a groove of good behavior and good choices without putting much thought into it. That isn't all bad. However, living purposefully is the only sure way to not slip into an unhealthy mentality. Habitual good behavior can gain the Lord's approval, which is nice, but awareness of potential pitfalls shows wisdom and purpose.

Planning wickedness is a choice, but many of God's children don't realize that the human condition defaults to sin. It takes wisdom to plan to do good; it's folly to leave planning on the back burner and just let things happen. That will lead into sin because a relationship with God takes effort, and a lack of effort leaves the soul undirected and vulnerable.

Lord Jesus, keep me holy. Guide my heart and remind me to keep my eyes focused on you.

Deep Roots

Wickedness never brings stability,
but the godly have deep roots.
PROVERBS 12:3 NLT

1 Peter 1:23 tells believers that we "have been born again, but not to a life that will quickly end. Your new life will last forever because it come from the eternal, living word of God." The Word of God is alive just like a seed is alive. It is perishable but enduring. That enduring quality means roots will grow. Give that seed water and sunlight, and it does grow. The roots sink deeply into the soul and send up shoots and fruits. We simply need to stay attentive and active.

Wickedness does not have the advantage of the authority of the King of kings. It is served by a fallen angel and has no stability. The children of God have a beautiful advantage; they serve the living God who plants seeds of truth and the enduring Word into our hearts and souls. We will learn and grow with the reading of the Word and the presence of the Holy Spirit within each of us.

Dear Lord, the Word is sweet and the seed obvious in my life. Thank you for nourishing the seed of your Word in me.

Be a Blessing

An excellent wife is the crown of her husband,
but she who brings shame is like rottenness in his bones.

PROVERBS 12:4 ESV

The Bible gives us many examples of how our behavior impacts others. When we act excellently, others are blessed. When we act shamefully, others are negatively impacted. An obvious example of this is in marriage, but the same could be said for any other relationship as well.

Children are impacted by their parents. We are all impacted by our friends, employers, and coworkers. There is a lot of value placed on relationships, and we should consider if we're a blessing or a curse to those closest to us.

Father, teach me to act nobly. I want my friends and family to be blessed by me and not burdened. Thank you for all the wonderful people you have put in my life.

Plan With Godliness

The plans of the godly are just;
the advice of the wicked is treacherous.
PROVERBS 12:5 NLT

Before making any plans, the first thing we should do as children of God is pray. Matthew 6:33 says, "Seek first the Kingdom of God above all else, and live righteously, and he will give you everything you need." When we pray, our hearts align with God's heart. We become vessels for his will to be done, and our desires become his desires, so we are more satisfied than we ever could be living in our ways.

When those who have rejected God give advice, they only have themselves to rely upon. They are not tapping into the wisdom of the ages, nor do they have the Spirit of the living God giving direction. It's not as dependable information or advice, and it can be dangerous to follow the words of these people. Sink deeply into the Word, pray diligently, and listen to the Holy Spirit when you plan.

Father, thank you for your direction and wisdom. I am grateful I can depend on you in every detail of my life from little things to life-changing plans.

Save Lives

The words of the wicked are like a murderous ambush,
but the words of the godly save lives.
PROVERBS 12:6 NLT

The most important decision Christians can make when listening to the advice of others is to purposefully discern the heart of the speaker. Sometimes it's difficult to weed out wisdom from noise. Today's verse tells us there are only two sides to this story: you are following the words of the godly, or the speaker is giving you the words of the wicked. The results are dichotomous: lives are saved with godly words, but murder comes from the mouths of those who listened to the evil one.

Don't rely only on words themselves to give insight. Words are just words unless they are in God's Bible. The condition of the speaker's heart will tell you if the words should be considered. Only the Word is pure and righteous, but the hearts of the godly strive toward Christian purity, and that is worthy of consideration.

Lord, give me discernment. Open my eyes and keep me holy. Soften my heart to the truth and beauty revealed in your Word through the people who live for you alone.

Godly Family

The wicked die and disappear,
but the family of the godly stands firm.
PROVERBS 12:7 NLT

The family of God often includes blood-related family, but God calls all who follow him his children. We are brothers and sisters, and that means more than blood. Jesus declared in Matthew 12:50, "Anyone who does the will of my Father in heaven is my brother and sister and mother." These are defined and important relationships. John later says in 1 John 2:9, "If anyone claims, 'I am living in the light,' but hates a fellow believer, that person is still living in darkness."

We need to take our relationships with other believers seriously. If we hate another believer, John says we're not saved. We're dead because hatred is death, and that's serious. Plead with the Lord to change hearts. There is strife among brothers and sisters worthy of our time and prayers.

Dear God, forgive me for any strife I have caused or been part of within the body of believers. Open my eyes to any hatred I may be harboring and please accept my repentance.

Sensibility Wins Admiration

A sensible person wins admiration,
but a warped mind is despised.
PROVERBS 12:8 NLT

The closer believers get to God, the more the world considers them strange and even warped. As our hearts and souls are purified by the living Word, we can depend on the conditions of our souls to the exclusion of unbelievers' opinions. We will become sensible; we will know truth. We will have wisdom and clarity.

Those who don't know God can't see the truth. We shouldn't be surprised at the depravity that overruns people who follow their own ways. They need to hear the Word of God, and we must keep our senses sharp so we can see opportunities to share the truth of Jesus with them. It's an honor and responsibility to be carrying the one true God in our hearts, and our job is to open doors to eternity whenever possible.

Keep me sharp, Father, to see when I can speak about you. Keep me aware of circumstances around me and hearts ready to hear the Word.

Ordinary Wins

Better to be an ordinary person with a servant
than to be self-important but have no food.
PROVERBS 12:9 NLT

There is glory in being normal and humble. In our humility, it isn't obvious whether we have a good standard of living, including enough to eat, but our circumstances are simple and never offensive. It is better to be stable in an ordinary way than to appear important but starve.

This is a bit of irony here. The person who doesn't want to admit any need is defeating himself with his own arrogance. He's starving while the humble person who glories in his own ordinariness is being served his dinner by his own servant. The desire to put up a front and pretend to have what doesn't exist is against the character of the Lord. Reputation is meaningless; humble integrity is better.

Lord, make me ordinary. Keep me humble despite my desire to protect my reputation. Please give me wisdom in handling my feelings about being transparent with others.

Care for Animals

The godly care for their animals,
but the wicked are always cruel.
PROVERBS 12:10 NLT

It's wonderful when we hear from the Lord that people, created in the image of the Almighty, should show his beautiful creatures special care and treatment as well. We can pay attention to how people treat their animals because that reveals their character.

God created animals with feelings even if they are temporary and immediate. They have repeatable and reliable instincts that have differences and similarities across the spectrum of species. They experience all the bodily issues that people do: things that bleed, break, and bulge. Animals are created for our blessing and our growth, and it makes sense that the godly will protect these precious creatures.

Father, thank you for the creatures in my life. Whether I see birds, woodland creatures, or wildlife out my window, or I have pets or livestock on my property, help me care for them properly.

Hard Workers Eat

A hard worker has plenty of food,
but a person who chases fantasies has no sense.
PROVERBS 12:11 NLT

There are many benefits to habitually working hard. In this verse, Solomon contrasts a hard worker to someone who chases fantasies. Abundance and sufficiency are directly related to how hard a person is willing to work. Part of this involves the type of work a person does, but hard work in and of itself is a blessing that provides provision and sustenance.

Fantasy-chasers are not working. Daydreaming slows work. There's no forward movement or income earned when people spend their time thinking and not putting those thoughts into actions. Paul put this principle into a personal perspective in 1 Corinthians 15:10, "Whatever I am now, it is all because God poured out his special favor on me—and not without results. For I have worked harder than any of the other apostles; yet it was not I but God who was working through me by his grace."

Father, please work through me as you worked through Paul. Make me into the person who serves you through hard work and attention to my relationship with you.

July

A gentle answer deflects anger,
but harsh words make tempers flare.

PROVERBS 15:1 NLT

Be Well Rooted

Thieves are jealous of each other's loot,
but the godly are well rooted and bear their own fruit.
PROVERBS 12:12 NLT

There's a lot to be said for being content in the Lord. When we are truly vested in what God says, then we inherently know whatever our income, wherever we live, and whomever we are living with are all blessings from God. These special components of our lives define how we live and what our daily experiences are composed of. We can lean into the Lord for each season of our lives and leave no room for jealousy.

If we have our eyes fixed firmly on God, we are not fixated on our neighbors. We are happy for others' blessings when we are content with our own. We know that where we now are is where the Lord wants us. We have a purpose and life, and we seek to fully live for his glory.

Lord, may I never know how a thief thinks or feels. May I sink into your will and your way. May I bear fruit for your kingdom and experience the blessings you have specifically for me.

Escape a Trap

The wicked are trapped by their own words,
but the godly escape such trouble.
Proverbs 12:13 NLT

How quickly we get ourselves into hot water with our words! If we're talking, we're not listening, and according to James 1:19, that's to our detriment. "Be quick to listen, slow to speak." And James doesn't stop there. In verses 22 and 25 he says, "Don't just listen to God's word. You must do what it says. Otherwise, you are only fooling yourselves…But if you look carefully into the perfect law that sets you free, and if you do what it says and don't forget what you heard, then God will bless you for doing it."

If we're busy reading the Word of God and listening to what he says, the tendency to override others with our own words lessens. We are challenged by the truth to make our words worthy of the kingdom and that keeps us from many troubles of this world.

Keep my mouth holy, Lord. Keep my words honoring to you and worthy of the kingdom. Let me be edifying to you alone.

Work and Wisdom

Wise words bring many benefits,
and hard work brings rewards.
PROVERBS 12:14 NLT

How do wise words bring benefits? Since wisdom comes from God alone, only by spending time with him and reading his Word can we become wise. When we speak wise words, we share the wisdom God has given us with others. God's comfort and understanding can spread through us to others. That benefits both us and them, and God is glorified.

Life is tough, and success will be found by those who work hard and are wise. The lazy and the foolish struggle because they are not going to God for encouragement and strength. Let's listen to God's truth, share it with others, and set an example of a godly work ethic by not growing weary.

Lord, renew me with strength to keep pressing forward in the responsibilities you have given to me. Please continue to impart your wisdom to me so I may share it with others and thereby glorify you.

Gift of Advice

The way of fools seems right to them,
but the wise listen to advice.
PROVERBS 12:15 NIV

Pride can impede our ability to learn and grow. We should care more about learning the truth than self-image. When others correct us or offer us advice, we can see it as a gift and an opportunity rather than an affront to our character. We have more to learn, but only the humble will. Instead of being so insistent on our way that we refuse to listen to any input from others, let's make a deliberate choice to remain approachable, teachable, and humble.

Ask for help when you need it. When someone disagrees with you, listen to what they are saying before you negate it. Put your pride aside and embrace learning. God designed us to need each other.

Please help me stay humble, Father God. When I am given the gift of advice, give me ears to hear and a heart to receive. It's sometimes hard to put my pride aside, but I want to continue to learn and grow.

Calm in the Storm

A fool is quick-tempered,
but a wise person stays calm when insulted.
PROVERBS 12:16 NLT

Our temperaments are the products of our spiritual states. The words in today's verse support the truth about temperaments. Our mouths reveal the conditions of our hearts, and there is little we can do about this. If we want to learn to curb our tongues, we first need to address the conditions of our hearts.

Wisdom seats itself in the heart. Knowledge is housed in the head. Knowledge is knowing how to write words and spell well; wisdom is judging when to use those words and for which purposes. Seek knowledge but understand the value and place of wisdom in the management of a person's path through life.

Lord, open my eyes to understand wisdom and keep my temperament within your glory. May my words show not just knowledge but also your wisdom.

Honest Witness

An honest witness tells the truth;
a false witness tells lies.
PROVERBS 12:17 NIV

Today's verse is straightforward. There's no gray area in Solomon's assessment; we are either for God or against him. We are either truth-tellers or liars. As children of God, we aspire to please him, and within the effort to please God and seek him is time spent reading the Word and praying. When we spend time with God in either of these pursuits, the seed of God's Word is planted our hearts. We are made new in the power of the Word. We are changed, and honesty is one of the characteristics of a changed heart.

We don't need to underestimate the power of the seed because we experience it firsthand. It's like losing weight. We will notice the first couple pounds gone while it might be days or weeks before someone else notices. When the seed of truth starts growing in us, we become aware of it almost immediately. The living God is amazing, and eternal life starts the moment the seed is planted.

Father, give me your living Word and grow me in honesty and integrity. Show me the way to your everlasting life.

Words Can Heal

Some people make cutting remarks,
but the words of the wise bring healing.
PROVERBS 12:18 NLT

If our hearts are not aligned with God, that will come out of our mouths. People who aren't checking their hearts with the Word might as well give up watching their tongues. The condition of our hearts reveals the direction of our eternal souls by the way we speak, the looks on our faces, and the attitudes we show to others.

When God says the Word became flesh in John 1:14, we start to see how important words are. God chose words as the vehicle for his truth and salvation. Our words are not living; only his have that power. God does speak through us to bring others to the kingdom, and if we are only interested in spouting our own drivel, we will miss opportunities to give the Lord room for his wisdom, honesty, and healing to come through our mouths.

Lord Jesus, speak through me. Use my words and heart to bring healing to a hurting world. Allow me to be your vessel.

Truth Doesn't Need Exposure

Truthful words stand the test of time,
but lies are soon exposed.
PROVERBS 12:19 NLT

Shakespeare had a way with words and knew a lot about them. In *The Merchant of Venice*, the character Lancelot famously said in Act 2, Scene 2, "The truth will out." That is what today's verse said fifteen hundred years before Shakespeare, but Solomon also added that truthful words will stand the test of time.

The pinnacle of truthful words is the Word of God. These were crafted by God through the work of approximately forty men over a span of fifteen hundred years. Over the course of time, the Bible has withstood countless attacks and rejections, and it still stands without any contradiction or errors within its pages. Between 1400 BC and 90 AD, every word was penned and preserved so we can access eternal glory.

Lord, belief is an act of trust in you. The further I go in my relationship with you, the more I love you and trust you with the entirety of my life. Thank you for giving me your truthful words.

Plan Peace

Deceit fills hearts that are plotting evil;
joy fills hearts that are planning peace!
Proverbs 12:20 NLT

It's a chicken-or-egg situation when we consider our hearts versus what we plan. Does the condition of the heart come first, or do we start planning and that determines the path our hearts take? Both are true. The condition of our hearts feeds the things we plan which feed the condition of our hearts. We are synergistic creations, and the Lord intended that from the beginning.

When our hearts wander or we are not focused on what we are saying or feeling, doing righteousness can bring us back to the correct path. We realign ourselves with God when we plan peaceful endeavors with positive results. On the other hand, if we make indulgent plans and follow through with only selfish desires, we will have momentary satisfaction and dire consequences. Checking the condition of the heart and keeping plans in the realm of peace will grow deeper relationships with God.

Purify my heart, Lord. When I get distracted or sidelined, remind me to plan with your peaceful ways and bring fruit back into my life. I will reflect on your goodness.

Attract No Harm

No harm comes to the godly,
but the wicked have their fill of trouble.
PROVERBS 12:21 NLT

This life is not the end of the story. So much of what Solomon discusses is in the realm of eternity. When we have our focus on everlasting life and not just the temporal life, our perspective shifts. Verses like today's start to make sense, and they bring hope and joy unlike anything else.

We can and likely will face persecution within this lifetime. We will be marginalized by people who don't love Christ or Christians, and this is extra painful if they are close friends or family. Persecution can have other consequences too. We can lose jobs, homes, or even our earthly lives because this world hates us and the one we serve. However, we have a firm foothold in heaven. We know where we're going. Our glory place is not now; it is with God, and it is eternal.

Dearest Lord, help me keep my perspective firmly in the future where I will sing praises and serve you forever. Thank you for your creation, but above all, thank you for you.

God's Delight

Lying lips are detestable to the L*ORD*,
but faithful people are his delight.
PROVERBS 12:22 CSB

We live in a culture that glorifies getting away with things, but are we getting away with them? God is the King of truth, so lying and deceiving are in direct opposition of him and his kingdom. When we lie, it's disgraceful to God. How can we represent him to anyone? The more we lie, the more callous our hearts become to it and the more our minds learn to justify it.

When we speak the truth and act faithfully, however, God delights in us. We can act like him and represent him to those around us even when it's difficult to tell the truth. If you have a habit of lying, it may require asking the Holy Spirit to expose your heart's intentions and uproot any lies you were told first. Whatever it takes, it's important to get back on God's path and walk in the way of truth.

God, forgive me for all the lies I've spoken. Please give me the strength to tell the truth when it's hard. I want to be like you and represent you well to others.

No Show Needed

The wise don't make a show of their knowledge,
but fools broadcast their foolishness.
PROVERBS 12:23 NLT

At some point in most of our lives, we start to realize we might not be as smart as we think we are. We only have our perspectives, and that is to our detriment. Once we realize the limitations of our single brains in a single moment in time, doors open.

All wisdom is from God. We are created by God. We have been invited to partake in an eternal life with God and in his wisdom by one path only. Through the blood of Christ and by way of repenting of our sins, our hearts and brains adapt to God's wisdom. New life in Christ changes us, and we couldn't know what we do now without him.

Jesus, keep me close. Hold me near and let me be with you. Some days, that is all I want. Make my thoughts your thoughts, make my words your words, and let me know your presence.

Diligence

Diligent hands will rule,
but laziness ends in forced labor.
PROVERBS 12:24 NIV

The Bible tells many stories of diligent, prayerful people who rose from a place of poverty into a role of leadership. Think of David, Joseph, Gideon, and Mary. There are also examples of people who failed to use their gifts or positions of power faithfully, and they were brought to ruin. Saul, Samson, Herod, or the lazy servant in Matthew 25 are examples.

If we spend all our effort and time chasing self-indulgence, God will take what he has trusted us with and give the responsibility to someone else. We will end up working harder, chasing our tails, rather than find ourselves in places of prominence with opportunities to create real change. Work is an opportunity to worship God and be part of what he's doing in the world. No work is menial in the kingdom of God; it all serves a purpose.

I delight in the work you have given me today, dear God. May my actions and efforts bring you praise and honor. Forgive me when I complain and teach me to be diligent.

Cheerful Words

Anxiety in a person's heart weighs it down,
but a good word cheers it up.
PROVERBS 12:25 CSB

Have you ever seen someone who looked so despondent, you wanted to say something to encourage them? Sometimes a little can go a long way. It may not fix the problem, but simply mentioning that you really appreciated what someone said or saying they look good in a certain color may help them smile and add a little cheer.

Perhaps there is a lot of weight on them and reminding them of simple truths could make a difference: "If you need anything, just let me know. We are one family in Christ," or "If you're feeling all alone right now, remember how much God cares about you. He's always nearby." Some days are more difficult than others, and that is why God has given us each other so we can pray for one another and offer cheerful words of encouragement.

Lord, please teach me what to say and when. I don't want to stay silent if I can encourage someone to keep going.

Give Good Advice

The godly give good advice to their friends;
the wicked lead them astray.
Proverbs 12:26 NLT

It's a hefty responsibility to be consulted for advice, and as believers, we need to be especially cautious. Advice takes one of two directions: it's either good or bad. This needs to be the first consideration before we open our mouths and give our thoughts to someone else about their circumstances.

Once done, however, and once we pray for wisdom that can only come from God, the floodgates fly open. We become vessels of truth with an eternal message for the suffering soul who needs the balm of God's Word. We need to speak at that point. We are in the exciting position of bringing beauty through the Word to a person who desperately needs it.

Open my mouth, dear Jesus, when my heart is right with you. Please close it and be firm with me when I am not speaking eternal truth to a loved one who needs to hear from you.

Use Everything

Lazy people don't even cook the game they catch,
but the diligent make use of everything they find.
PROVERBS 12:27 NLT

It's tragic when the death of an animal does not bless the life of a person. Caring for animals, even the ones killed for food, is mentioned in Proverbs 12:10. The lazy person has no excuse in the Lord's eyes. If they kill, they must dress the meat and prepare the meal that should come from the forfeited life of that animal.

Some cultures wisely use most parts of a kill for something useful for their survival. Native people around the globe use all parts and pieces from the outside of an animal, like leather for clothing and bowls, to the inside for tendons and sinews as thread and bowstrings. Nothing is wasted, and every bit is considered a precious resource. That level of diligence is what the Lord is asking of us. Don't miss blessings because you are too lazy to put in the work to find them.

Please forgive my laziness, Father. I sometimes struggle to work when I would rather indulge myself. Give me motivation and grace to use everything.

Leads to Life

The way of the godly leads to life;
that path does not lead to death.
PROVERBS 12:28 NLT

Day by day, we walk through the blessing of life. Each moment falls upon the last, and we are sometimes overwhelmed by the responsibility of being believers. We know doing good is the result of a saved soul, but sometimes the doing-good part becomes the focus. That is where the soul suffers or becomes waylaid.

Nothing is gained when we rely upon our personal strength to get us through life. We live for one reason and one reason only: for Christ. He is our blessing and purpose. He is where we go when we need energy and a zest for life. He gives us direction and clarity. When things are overwhelming and unclear, he is the answer.

Dear God, open my eyes to the direction you have chosen for me. Keep me energized when I do your will and willing to plow through the tough parts when you convict me.

A Parent's Discipline

A wise child accepts a parent's discipline;
a mocker refuses to listen to correction.
PROVERBS 13:1 NLT

Learning from our heavenly Father is the height of wisdom, and Solomon knew God was his Father. It's especially prudent to accept the Father's discipline, although most people would first pause before realizing or appreciating the disciple that is happening to them. Proverbs 3:11-12 tells us everyone God loves is disciplined, and we're not to hate it or get tired of it. Discipline affirms we are God's children!

King David is a great example for us. He was loved by God, but he still messed up. His reaction to God's discipline is a good lesson for us. In Psalm 38, he doesn't want to be disciplined, but he accepts it. He's overwhelmed by pain; he's sick with a fever and his wounds are infected as a consequence of some unknown action. No one wants to get what he has, and they stay away, so he's lonely. He's got a lot of enemies who are enjoying the fact that he's falling apart, and he begs God to stay close.

Dear Lord, please help me recognize discipline from you. I want to learn from your eternal lessons and depend on you.

Guard the Mouth

Whoever guards his mouth preserves his life;
he who opens wide his lips comes to ruin.
PROVERBS 13:3 ESV

One of the first lessons a wise Christian can learn is to be quiet and listen. So much is gained if we wait to speak because there are many people we can learn from. Wisdom isn't just a dose of spirituality and you're good to go. Wisdom is a lengthy, earth-moving personality shift. It takes time and energy to acquire it, but the blessing of that work is a preserved life.

The quickest way to dispel thoughts of being wise is to open our mouths and speak. If we had any illusions that we are truly tapping into God's wisdom, talking quickly without thinking or praying first is humbling. We don't understand God or his wisdom if we assume we are wise just because we are believers. God works with us, on us, and through us for ages and ages, and one day, we realize we have nothing worthy to say. That's wisdom.

Father God, make me and break me so I can be more like you. Quiet my soul so I can hear you and others who know better than I do.

Desires of the Diligent

A sluggard's appetite is never filled,
but the desires of the diligent are fully satisfied.
PROVERBS 13:4 NIV

When we hunger and thirst for righteousness, Jesus says in Matthew 5:6 that he will fill us up. When we seek goodness and God, we will have eternal satisfaction. There is nothing like it. Answers to eternal questions—the meaning of life, or where we go after this one—are only satisfied by the truth spoken by God. No other answers will satisfy because they fall short of the truth. They stir the soul seeking absolute glory. God is the only answer.

When we don't take the time or effort to seek the truth about our eternal destiny, there never will be any satisfaction. There can't be fulfillment if we don't look for answers. There is only one way to God, and that is through the broken, bloodied body of Jesus Christ and his resurrection for our redemption. If we don't seek him, we won't find him. If we don't find him, we will live eternally without him, and that is an eternal wasteland.

Father, let me be satisfied in you, and let me be diligent in seeking you. Reveal your truth and answer all questions. Thank you so much for the peace and satisfaction that comes from knowing the truth.

Any Deception

Some people pretend to be rich but really have nothing.
Others pretend to be poor but really are wealthy.
PROVERBS 13:7 NCV

Deceit, especially self-deceit, is the saddest of lies. People who pretend to be something they are not usually lie to themselves first and then everyone around them as well. The lies become entrenched into a bizarre, precarious life form. It takes work to keep this pretense propped up and turned on. It takes money, time, and a lot of other resources. It also robs a person of the rich, wonderful relationships and experiences that the pretense drains from daily life.

There's nothing more freeing or refreshing than living a transparent life. It's lovely to live with complete honesty, never make excuses, and not worry how others perceive us. Honest living gives us time to focus on the needs of others. We can have long conversations or take meals to the sick and overwhelmed. When we live with eternity as our focus, all we are and have become resources for God's kingdom.

Lord, take my life and be glorified. I have nothing to offer but myself, and I pray I can serve you throughout my life.

The Ransom

The ransom of a man's life is his wealth,
but a poor man hears no threat.
PROVERBS 13:8 ESV

When we own a lot of stuff, it owns us. Cleaning and maintenance take up time and money. We need to spend time on stuff, or it will disintegrate or go bad. If we don't clean it, it will smell and degrade. No matter how we look at it, time spent with stuff is time not spent with people. Heaven is populated with people, not stuff.

There's no doubt that some stuff is a blessing. It's great to have a bed and a lamp. Books are an amazing blessing. Food is wonderful. Clothing is essential. A warm house in the winter; protection from the sun in the summer. Beyond these essentials, we need to question what is blessing and what is a burden. If people are hovering around and demanding our stuff, maybe owning less is a good answer so we can focus on what people really need.

Lord, my God, please bless me with enough but not too much. Help me live a life of balance and beauty so I am a testament to you no matter what I own.

Light and Joy

The life of the godly is full of light and joy,
but the light of the wicked will be snuffed out.
PROVERBS 13:9 NLT

Heaven will be amazing. If the world is a glimpse of glory, we're in for a treat in eternity. We get to live now with the Holy Spirit in us and together with Jesus, and we get to spend forever in the presence of God. We read in Revelation 21:4 that we will live without tears, pain, or death. God's house has many rooms, and Revelation 4:6 tell of a sea of glass that is near God's throne. Heaven will be beautiful beyond anything conceivable now.

The life of an unbeliever is snuffed out; a wicked person will die eternally. There is no light or joy. There is no sea of glass or a house with many rooms. Like a candle whose flame has been snuffed, a wicked person's life will go out and that's it. With the help of the Holy Spirit, we can reach out to them first.

Lord, may my life be full of light, joy, and purpose driven by your Holy Spirit. May I be a bright candle for others to find their way to you.

Wisdom Takes Advice

Where there is strife, there is pride,
but wisdom is found in those who take advice.
PROVERBS 13:10 NIV

It's an old saying; a person has two ears, two eyes, and one mouth for a reason. We need to speak half as much, or less, as we look or listen. Eyes and ears are open; mouth is closed. That's the right position for us to learn humility; we hear others speak, and we find out how much they know. We hear about other experiences, lives lived far away, and different family and relationship dynamics. We learn about career moves and job experiences we will never know, and we learn. We hear how people think and communicate differently.

Listening to others is a good way to avoid pride. When we are observant enough to see pain, joy, and stress, we become God's messengers. When we realize everyone has a story and there's a lesson in each one, we become students. We don't add strife to relationships when we are truly hearing the one who speaks.

Speak through me, God, and keep me humble. Open my ears so I can hear what is truly going on in other lives.

Easy Money

Money that comes easily disappears quickly,
but money that is gathered little by little will grow.
PROVERBS 13:11 NCV

It would be less challenging a life if money didn't exist, but here we are. Money determines most life's physical choices while God's Word persistently tells us to get our spiritual lives in order by not focusing on money. One of the hardest things to do is to let go of a focus on money and determinedly nurture a focus on God. Today's verse tells us a simple fact about money; if it comes easily, it will also go easily. A slow, determined path to increasing our wealth assures growth. That's God's wisdom through the very wealthy King Solomon, and we would do well to listen.

As God's people, he intends for us to work consistently and diligently to acquire the fruits of our labor. We will see growth. The days become weeks which become years, and the growth of money demonstrates to us how we acquire wisdom, love, tenacity, and more of God's characteristics.

Grow me, God. Let me be responsible for showing others your kingdom through the management of my money.

Revere the Commandment

Whoever despises the word brings destruction on himself,
but he who reveres the commandment will be rewarded.
PROVERBS 13:13 ESV

God doesn't have much patience for those who despise him. There will be no blessings or graces vested in the lives of people who hate the Word of God. It's important these people know whom they are fighting. Do they realize the Creator of the universe will only see them destroyed? There's nothing there but grief and pain.

The children of God will experience the opposite as we are showered with blessings and rewards. We have the love of God to protect us and the Holy Spirit to guide us. We are assured of no pain and no suffering when we get to heaven; we are given the presence of our Lord forever. If we can grasp what that means, we can marvel in ways that exemplify that experience.

Open my eyes to how mighty you are, Father. Let me grasp your power and glory. Let me speak boldly to people who hate your Word in a way that shows your love for them.

Avoid Snares

The instruction of the wise is like a life-giving fountain;
those who accept it avoid the snares of death.
PROVERBS 13:14 NLT

In the book of John, Jesus encountered a Samaritan woman at a well. Since she came from a people despised by the Jews, she did not expect Jesus to talk to her, let alone have a conversation. By showing her acceptance and love despite her sinful life and ostracized group, Jesus gave her an important message. The water she hauled up from the well would still leave a person thirsty sometime after drinking; Jesus is the eternal spring of water, and no one will thirst again if they drink from that truth.

Wisdom comes from God. There is no true wisdom without him, and therefore we can trust him to be the life-giving fountain. The living water gives us the one and only path through those snares. He is truth and love.

Father, I love and need you. Thank you for giving me the truth of your Word. Thank you for giving me you.

Good Understanding

People with good understanding will be well liked,
but the lives of those who are not trustworthy are hard.
PROVERBS 13:15 NCV

When we lean into the Almighty, we tap into the truth and light he offers. Our dependency on him allows truth and light to shine through us so others can find their way to a relationship with God. We grasp that special understanding which opens the door to wisdom, and we are then worthy vessels for the Lord. People who are not yet believers may not be aware why they like the integrity and understanding of believers, but that attraction can plant an eternal seed.

People who close the door to the goodness and light offered through God's people choose a thorny path. Their lives will be hard. They will stumble, relationships will be broken, and the way will be dark. When God's people come alongside these dark souls with understanding and light, they can offer the path to heaven.

Dear Jesus, make me grasp understanding and see the truth. Let me be your light; teach me how to best show your grace to others.

Prudent Knowledge

All who are prudent act with knowledge,
but fools expose their folly.
PROVERBS 13:16 NIV

As the saying says, it pays to be informed. A prudent person spends time learning. They wisely choose how they spend their time, and there's purpose and reservation in their choices. This all leads to a personality that acts in wisdom; they act with the Holy Spirit moving through them.

You could choose to hide your light under a bushel as told in Matthew 15:15, but it's hard to hide that you're a fool. That leaks out of every pore. Perhaps things come out of the mouth that shouldn't be said, behavior is questionable, or life is on a downward spiral. Believers would do well to study the Word as an effective way to avoid being a fool while showing patience to unbelievers who exhibit this behavior.

Lord, make me wise. Keep me from being a fool. Help me know your ways and be prudent.

Reliable Messenger

An unreliable messenger stumbles into trouble,
but a reliable messenger brings healing.
PROVERBS 13:17 NLT

We are messengers for God; we deliver the Word to each other and to the lost. We are given the Word so we can grow characteristics that feed reliability. We grow diligence and forthrightness. We gain wisdom and insight; we show compassion and honesty. These qualities bring healing. The calmness and serenity of a Christian with these qualities will lower tensions and heighten the kindness of others.

On the other hand, unreliability increases anxiety. It mismanages the Word of God. We can't risk being people who misrepresent God and his Word. In Ephesians 2:10 we read that "we are God's masterpiece. He has created us anew in Christ Jesus, so we can do the good things he planned for us long ago." We can be reliable messengers because he equipped us to be so, but only if we rely on him and understand our position as his creation.

Dear Lord, I love that I need you and that you love me for it. Thank you for our relationship. You are the most important relationship I have.

Heeding Correction

Whoever disregards discipline comes to poverty and shame,
but whoever heeds correction is honored.
PROVERBS 13:18 NIV

There are a multitude of people willing to share their so-called wisdom with us, but only those who learn from the Word of God are worth heeding. Being corrected is a lifelong need, but discernment is gained when we read the Word and pray for wisdom. Everyone God loves receives discipline through their lives, but it's important to recognize what is from the Lord and what is unnecessary noise.

A lack of discipline will end in poverty and shame, and shame from God is true shame. The truth will be made known by the Almighty when he decides it is time. We, his children, need to heed him. God has declared what will happen, and we who love him will be by his side. Pray for those who are not yet destined to be there.

Father, may I rest in your presence and heed your discipline. May I love your correction and revel in your careful watch over me.

August

A friend is always loyal,
and a brother is born to help
in time of need.

PROVERBS 17:17 NLT

Wishes Come True

It is so good when wishes come true,
but fools hate to stop doing evil.
PROVERBS 13:19 NCV

As we give our hearts to the Lord, we change. We become new in Jesus, and what we wish for lines up with his desires for us. When our wishes align with God's, it's not too surprising when they come true! He loves to bless us, and he loves to give us our hearts' desires when we are dedicated to him.

People who don't love God or don't follow his Word are foolish. They persist in rebelling against God, and they keep doing evil. They unwisely indulge in momentary entertainments and bypass the living God for their own pleasure. God gives fully to those of us who love him. May our lives be a witness to an eternity with him.

Dear Lord, keep me close so I can know your goodness. Let me know the wishes of your heart for me so they will come true.

Righteous Rewarded

Disaster pursues sinners,
but the righteous are rewarded with good.
PROVERBS 13:21 ESV

There is a difference between being a sinner and being a sinner who has repented. When we give our lives over to God, we repent of all our sins, and we are made new. The motivations of our hearts change, and we reflect the King as we grow closer to him. The Lord blesses us when we pursue him. He pursues us as well, and we have a wonderful, synergistic relationship with the Almighty that shines light and glory around us. This is truly a supernatural experience.

When we live as unrepentant sinners, there is no redemption. We continue to live for only ourselves and our selfish desires, and we don't give God the opportunity to change our hearts and the path of our lives. We remain destined for eternity without our loving God, and that is tragic. As today's verse tells us, it's a disaster. We need our Redeemer to change the course of life for us. We need to be forgiven so we can be one of the righteous rewarded with his goodness.

Dear Father, I love to be near you. I love to know you and learn more about you in your Word. Thank you for your transformative love.

A Sinner's Wealth

Good people leave their wealth to their grandchildren,
but a sinner's wealth is stored up for good people.
PROVERBS 13:22 NCV

In the end, God's children are rewarded, and those who reject the Lord will be punished. That's enough motivation to speak often about his grace. We receive unimaginable wealth from God as we submit our lives to him. He redeems us and blesses us in unexpected and beautiful ways in our daily lives. All he asks is that we forfeit ourselves to follow him. In the process, we find unimaginable joy and satisfaction.

Some people who reject God have worldly wealth. Unfortunately for them, it's temporary and worth nothing in heaven. Eternity is for glory, and the wealth of this world looks different from there. As we keep our eyes on Jesus, we become wealthy in a heavenly way. An unbeliever's wealth is eternally meaningless, but a believer's wealth will bless generations.

Father, make me wealthy where it counts. May I be a Christian who understands wealth from your perspective.

An Unplowed Field

An unplowed field produces food for the poor,
but injustice sweeps it away.
PROVERBS 13:23 NIV

It's grievous to see the abundance from our work go to waste. It's even worse to see it swept away in purposeful disregard for the money, time, and effort spent producing the crop. What we love is gone. Our work is purposeless, and it's sad to know we don't have value. Injustice does that to people. Life's work is disregarded, and people become meaningless.

When we have an abundance to share with others, it's joyful. We feel God's grace washing through us and into the lives of those around us. We feel grateful to be vessels for God in his pursuit of people for his kingdom and his care of his children. God is so good in his tenderness and love. We are blessed when he blesses others through us.

Lord, thank you for using me and my abundance for your glory. Being a member of your kingdom in this way is an unbelievable honor.

Belly of the Wicked

The godly eat to their hearts' content,
but the belly of the wicked goes hungry.
PROVERBS 13:25 NLT

When we join God's family, we eat at the table with him. We gather and share our blessings, and they overflow for each other. Our hearts are full when we do God's work. He cares and nurtures us as he moves us toward eternity with him. Contentment from God is not something we can imagine before we become believers. He fills us up. He gives us eternity; he is our all in all. It's unimaginable until it is experienced.

That gnawing hunger as an unbeliever is irrepressible. It consumes us from the inside out. We are never fulfilled, and we are always searching. Unbelievers keep reaching for and not quite grasping something they can't recognize. May we patiently and persistently give the Word to those seeking. May we remember how it was to not believe, and may we never forget for the sake of those who need God and haven't submitted to him yet.

Lord, I love you and need you. I want to give your truth to any who will listen. Please keep me alert and ready to speak about you.

God's Process

Hope deferred makes the heart sick,
But when the desire comes, it is a tree of life.
PROVERBS 13:12 NKJV

Everyone wants things, but God has a process. He wants us to accompany him on a journey of faith. He does not want to tease or torture us; he wants us to grow and mature into unstoppable, hopeful, faithful people who cannot be uprooted or derailed. He wants to give us more than we expect and better than we imagine. Sometimes the process seems endless, but when our desires are finally fulfilled in the most amazing, timely ways, we see why the wait was best.

We are not in control when we surrender our lives to God. When we enter faith, we acknowledge God's way is best and his timing impeccable. There is much to learn in the difficult days of waiting that can't be learned any other way. Let go of the reins and trust your heavenly Father. It may take longer than you wanted, but you will not be disappointed.

More than anything else, God, I desire you. Please refine and fulfill my other desires according to your will.

Life Companions

He who walks with wise men will be wise,
But the companion of fools will be destroyed.
PROVERBS 13:20 NKJV

There is a difference between loving all people in the name of Christ and selecting your walking companions. Those who you listen to, who walk through life with you, who fill your free time and share your ideas are the people you will become more like. If your closest companions are making bad choices, complaining and cursing, and studying the world instead of the Word, they will eventually lead you astray as well.

It is paramount to surround yourself with wise people who will challenge you, hold you accountable to your goals and morals, and get you excited about the things of God. The Bible warns us, "Evil company corrupts good habits" (1 Corinthians 15:33), so make sure the company you keep feeds your good habits and not your bad ones.

God, please bring wise people into my life who will help me keep my good habits.

Discipline

Whoever spares the rod hates his son,
but he who loves him is diligent to discipline him.
PROVERBS 13:24 ESV

How we respond to discipline or correction says a lot about our maturity. Children tend to disrespect parents or teachers who won't discipline them. Even though they fight discipline when it's enforced, they tend to gravitate to, trust, and respect their parents and teachers who insist on good behavior. When rules and consequences are insisted upon, children know they are safe, they matter, and they're capable of rising to the occasion.

As God's children, we know he disciplines us because he loves us and is calling us to a higher level of expectation. Like children, we flourish under loving discipline because it matures us and teaches us the best way to live. With God's help and humble hearts, let's respond positively and faithfully both in receiving and giving discipline.

Your righteous discipline, Father, conveys to me your message of love. Please teach me how to accept and lovingly administer discipline.

Seems Right

There is a way that seems right to a man,
but its end is the way of death.
PROVERBS 14:12 ESV

It is good for believers to acknowledge early on that we, in human wisdom, are easily led astray. We think things are good, but we only have ourselves to rely on. Human perception is faulty at best and dangerous at worst. We lack wisdom, the experience of the ages, and a heavenly perspective. What we don't have, God does.

The way of the Lord leads to life; the way of self-deception leads to death. It may seem black and white, but eternity will be spent in the light or in the dark. We have the choice throughout our lives to decide the path. The way may seem right, but it isn't unless God is intimately involved in our every step. Surety belongs to God, and the way to heaven is only through him.

Father, convict me of the righteous path and open my eyes to my deceptions. May truth be foremost in my life.

Stay Out of Trouble

Wise people are careful and stay out of trouble,
but fools are careless and quick to act.
PROVERBS 14:16 NCV

Care takes work and attention. Avoiding trouble is a purposeful decision, and it can't be done haphazardly. Trouble happens when little or no effort is put into life's moments. Big trouble happens when we let life just happen without any thought about potential outcomes.

Diligent, thoughtful planning is required when we accept salvation from God. We no longer get to ignore signs and nudging from the Holy Spirit. God expects us to attend to him, serve him, and learn from him. He wants us to keep our focus so we will be blessed. The wide path and its inherent troubles await us when we are careless and quick to act without listening and praying to our loving Lord. The narrow path and its amazing blessings are ours if we look to the Word and our amazing Father for deliverance and guidance.

Dear Lord, please teach me how to lean on you. Show me your ways of caution and thoughtfulness. Grow me to be closer to you and willing to listen.

Quick Tempers

A man of quick temper acts foolishly,
and a man of evil devices is hated.
PROVERBS 14:17 ESV

Volatile behavior has found some credibility in modern culture. People are following influencers who exhibit everything from the inappropriate to the profane. It's changing society. It's changing standards.

When we trust in the Lord and diligently learn from his Word, we can avoid the world's accepted, but incorrect, standards. The Bible holds everything we need: truth about being human, living in society, interactions and relationships, and more. As our hearts become fertile soil for the Word of God to sprout and grow, we learn God's expectations which are the same now as they always have been and will be. It's comforting to know the King of forever tells us everything we need to know.

My King and God, I submit my behavior to you. Please teach me to know what is acceptable in your sight.

Prudent Crowned

Simpletons are clothed with foolishness,
but the prudent are crowned with knowledge.
PROVERBS 14:18 NLT

It's not a crime to have any level of intelligence, but it is a crime to not use the intelligence God gave each of us. When the Holy Spirit moves in our hearts and minds, we change. Whether we're highly intellectual or much simpler in our thinking, if we learn the Word and give control to the Almighty, he will give us the knowledge and discernment we need to be wise.

It's easy to give ourselves over to foolishness. We don't have to make any effort to learn from God because we come clothed in the Son right from the beginning. However, diligence in knowing God will make us prudent and wise, and the Lord then promises a crown of knowledge. What grace!

Lord, equip and ready me to follow you through this life with your crown on my head. Teach me when and what to speak and give me wisdom for your glory only.

Mercy Makes Happiness

He who despises his neighbor sins;
But he who has mercy on the poor, happy is he.
PROVERBS 14:21 NKJV

It's a good decision to get along with our neighbors. Proximity can be a blessing in daily life as well as in times of trouble. Solomon goes a step further and tells us it's a sin to hate our neighbors. We know hating anyone is a sin, but hating a neighbor is highlighted in today's proverb. Solomon focused on neighbors for the role they play in our lives.

Neighbors are probably not family, and they are not necessarily friends. They may or may not be acquaintances, but we can offer our neighbors resources for home, yard, time, and energy. It's amazing avenue for speaking about God when we interact over things we own and can share. Grace with those who aren't close can be a real test of character, but by leaning into God, we can show his love throughout the neighborhood. And if we are the ones borrowing, we can be people of integrity and be prompt with returning and replacing.

Thank you for my neighbors, Lord Jesus. Help me show them your love through my resources and time.

Loved and Trusted

Those who make evil plans will be ruined,
but those who plan to do good will be loved and trusted.
PROVERBS 14:22 NCV

Few people would prefer evil being done to them rather than good. Earth swings toward evil on the societal spectrum, but when it comes to a personal level, there are few who would choose a slap on the face over chocolate cake. On the other hand, there are many people who enjoy doing evil rather than good.

The discrepancy conjures up the Golden Rule: "Do to others what you would want them to do to you" found in Luke 6:31. That levels the playing field, but Jesus wants us to take that further. In Matthew 5, he says to turn the other cheek if someone slaps us; if someone wants our shirt, give them the coat too; if someone wants us to go a mile with them, go two. The way to do good is beyond our thoughts of being nice to people. Jesus wants us to extend kindness toward evil doers.

Lord, I know I'm not capable of being gracious in the face of evil. Please move me in ways only you can.

Works Means Profit

Work brings profit,
but mere talk leads to poverty!
PROVERBS 14:23 NLT

As much as many people like to talk, few get paid to do so! Most of us need to work other jobs to have the necessities of life. Good work engages body and soul. Whether it's a desk job with lots of repetition or complex thinking, or a physical job with lots of activity and required strength, work is a blessing. The apostle Paul instructed the people in the church in Ephesus, "Use your hands for good hard work, and then give generously to others in need." There's good reason to work aside from sustaining ourselves; we get the opportunity to show Jesus' love and generosity to others.

People who talk but don't work won't have resources to spare. When Solomon said, we can assume he was not speaking about Scripture. Those who tell others about the Word are doing valuable work which is the opposite of mere talk. Work is a blessing, and the Lord affirms that.

Thank you, Lord, for the work you have brought me.

Wisdom Makes Wealth

Wise people are rewarded with wealth,
but fools only get more foolishness.
PROVERBS 14:24 NCV

Foolishness is a mindset that spirals into itself; wisdom spins heavenward as it builds. We will live in one direction or the other. The choices we make throughout our lives will dictate our method and path. We will each choose to take the steps downward or heavenward. From a distant view, many choices could go either way, but the heart of a wise person will be led by the Lord to the correct conclusion.

We don't get to decide our standards and our own "right" thing. Our Father is a deity of absolutes. There is a right path and a wrong path. There are variations within that narrow, right path, but the Lord delineates what is right and wrong in Scripture. When we read and know what he says, we have the ultimate guide for life.

Father, sharpen my mind and soften my heart so I can hear and know your Word. It means everything to have your presence guiding me.

Safety and Security

Those who fear the LORD are secure;
he will be a refuge for their children.
PROVERBS 14:26 NLT

The fear God wants us to feel for him is a respect that sends us running to him when times are tough. It's not fear that drives us to hide from him and try our luck in this world alone. He is a loving Father who will not be disrespected, but he will also do everything to protect us.

He is our refuge, strength, clear direction, and answer to confusion. His commandments were written to help guide and teach us. The world tries to confuse, tempt, and ultimately destroy us, but God offers us safety and security with him.

God, you have put rules in place for my benefit: for my safety, growth, and potential. Thank you for being the perfect Father and for leading me in love.

Fountain of Life

The fear of the LORD is a fountain of life,
that one may turn away from the snares of death.
PROVERBS 14:27 ESV

The way of the Lord leads to a fountain that promises eternal life; it is not a trail riddled with deadly snares. It's a joy to follow God. He brings out beauty in the world around us and gives us eyes to see it. He allows us to hear creation in all its seasonal glory so we can be awed by him. We glimpse him and heaven by observing this earth with eternity in mind. We see God when we look at what he has made.

It all starts with a good, healthy fear of the Lord. We will see glory if we understand how awesome and fearsome our Creator is. If we acknowledge his power, knowing he is the overcomer of all evil, we start to understand the God we serve. He is mightier than all that exists. He is our omniscient Father.

Oh Father, I am grateful for you. I am in awe of your power and might, and I bow down to your everlasting glory.

Patience

Whoever is patient has great understanding,
but one who is quick-tempered displays folly.
PROVERBS 14:29 NIV

When we act hastily, we often make decisions not aligned with the heart of God. Sarah desperately gave Hagar to Abraham to have a son instead of waiting for God to fulfill his promise to her in Genesis 16:1-2, hungry Esau impulsively traded away his birthright for a bowl of stew in Genesis 25:29-34, and Moses impatiently struck a rock when God told him only to speak to it in Numbers 20:7-12. All these instances led to complicated outcomes which ran contrary to God's plan.

Impatience reveals a lack of trust; patience leads to understanding and favorable outcomes. Christ displayed incredible patience, and he still does with us today. Practicing patience is honoring to God, beneficial for us, and leads to breakthrough in our faith and lives. Let's practice patience today.

When I feel worried or impatient, Lord God, please remind me of your faithfulness. Teach me to trust you more.

Sound Heart

A sound heart is life to the body,
But envy is rottenness to the bones.
PROVERBS 14:30 NKJV

The health of the body consumes a lot of time, energy, and attention in our culture, but Christians should also be aware of the body's connection to the soul. What we choose to believe doesn't just have eternal consequences; there are temporal consequences too. The condition of our hearts isn't just a matter of eating heart-healthy food. It's also important to put the God of love first in our thinking and purpose.

When we place him first, we calm ourselves, we are more aware of our surroundings, and we're focused on others. These decisions lead to a longer life. If we are consumed by greed and envy, we bring anger and negativity into our thoughts. That will shorten our breaths, tighten our stomachs, and increase stress. This will, according to today's verse, be rottenness to the bones which is a poetic way to say those thoughts will shorten a life.

Dear God, give me a healthy body so I can serve you longer and bring joy to those around me. I pray for good health rather than dependency on others if it is your will.

Help the Poor

Those who oppress the poor insult their Maker,
but helping the poor honors him.
PROVERBS 14:31 NLT

We can take one direction or the other. We are either ignoring the poor, or we are helping them. One choice insults God, and the other honors him. The Bible calls God our Maker in this verse. It's eye-opening to acknowledge our Father is the Maker of each of us. Whether we are poor or paying the bills with ease, we are made in God's image by his specific design. We are precious to him, and he wants us to treat each other as precious as well.

Helping the poor is not necessarily a demand on the wallet. We can help in soup kitchens, donate clean clothing, or teach a skill that could lead to employment. We can hire people who don't have an income or give rides to those who can't afford a vehicle. These purposeful and kind activities honor God because they honor the people who need help the most.

Maker, make me aware of people who need a hand with anything. Keep me prepared and willing in my schedule and in my heart.

Protected in Death

The wicked are ruined by their own evil,
but those who do right are protected even in death.
PROVERBS 14:32 NCV

Christians know there is an afterlife, and we know where we will spend it. God's design protects us both now and eternally. We will not be overcome by human evil or the ways of the devil. God has given us his Word to learn from and his Holy Spirit to dwell in us and guide us, and he will be with us all our days. We are one with the Spirit, and we are one with Christ. As children of the living God, we have a hedge of divine protection around us.

For those who reject a relationship with God, there is only one way, and it leads to ruin. Life will be disappointing or painful or both. There will be little satisfaction for those who don't serve God because all that is left is serving themselves or living as purposeless do-gooders. It is life changing to serve an almighty god who wants us to be with him in glory forever. A pain-free, satisfying eternity awaits those who live righteously for God.

May my life be for your glory, God. May my days be filled with righteousness and wisdom so your purpose will be obvious to any who look at me.

Where Wisdom Rests

Wisdom rests in the heart of him who has understanding,
But what is in the heart of fools is made known.
PROVERBS 14:33 NKJV

We reflect God when we speak to people with kindness and understanding. We can't hide the presence of the Holy Spirit when he dwells in us and exists in the words we speak and the demeanor we present. Those we speak to and anyone listening in will see the care and concern in what is said, but they will also find out about Jesus if they pursue the power behind the words.

The Lord is the source of wisdom. When we belong to him, we tap into that wisdom as we learn more about him and his Word. Our lives reflect the King of kings in ways we can't when we are void of the Holy Spirit. Before we were wise, we were fools. It isn't criticism; it's fact. It takes patience and understanding to speak about God to those who don't know him yet. It takes kindness to understand that unbelievers, without the Holy Spirit in them, can't know wisdom.

Father, fill my heart with understanding. Allow me to tell others about you with a kindness that overrides any foolishness. Open my heart to your Spirit moving though me.

Exalting the Nation

Righteousness exalts a nation,
but sin is a reproach to any people.
PROVERBS 14:34 ESV

Doing right is the way to more blessings than we can imagine. We are blessed with growing integrity. Our families are blessed with our wisdom and diligence. Our communities are blessed with the presence of strong family units and the healthy, trustworthy children that often grow up in such families. Nations are blessed with communities that have strong economies and generous, hard-working citizens.

Sin erodes such blessings. It decreases the effective work of those who indulge in it. It undermines families, and when the family unit is weakened in any community, it spreads resources thinner and puts more demands on others. God's way is the best way on so many levels of society, but it starts with individual people deciding to put God first in their lives. It's important to keep our eyes on God and make each decision for him.

Make my steps matter, Father. Keep me a strong citizen of heaven so I can be a blessing to my family, my community, and my country.

Gentle Answer

A gentle answer will calm a person's anger,
but an unkind answer will cause more anger.
Proverbs 15:1 NCV

When Daniel and his three friends were forced into slavery, their morals were tested. They did not believe it was right for them to eat the king's meat or delicacies. Instead of stubbornly refusing, they petitioned to eat their own, healthier food and explained how it would help them serve the king better. Because of their humble attitude and well-crafted rationale, their request was granted.

God's way proved to be the best way because Daniel and his friends were healthier and stronger than the others. They were able to follow God's commands, bring positive attention to God's better way of doing things, and not incite the king's rage, all because they used a kind and gentle answer. They could have been righteously persecuted for stubborn choices, but they found a better way of addressing the problem which saved their lives and impacted the kingdom.

I want to learn your better ways, dear God. Even if I'm right, I can become wrong by giving way to anger. Please help me keep my answers kind, calm, and gentle so I don't stir up unnecessary anger.

Joy and Sorrow

A glad heart makes a cheerful face,
but by sorrow of heart the spirit is crushed.
PROVERBS 15:13 ESV

Joy and sorrow run deeper than happiness and sadness. Joy and sorrow are heart conditions, and our faces and attitudes can't help but reflect what is in our hearts. We have happy moments and sad moments, but we can keep God's joy tucked inside our hearts, so we're never undone by passing pleasures or disappointments.

A sorrowful person lives crushed and defeated; that is not the inheritance of a child of God. He has endless joy available for us, and that's how he wants us to live. How much more beautiful and inviting is a person who has a smile on their face? We're not expected to pretend happiness or force a smile when we are down, but when the unexplainable joy of the Lord fills your heart, it will radiate through your countenance.

Following you fills me with joy, dear Jesus. This joy affects my attitude, my life, and even my appearance. I can't thank you enough for giving me your joy which supersedes all other fleeting feelings.

Little Is Better

Better is a little with the fear of the LORD,
Than great treasure with trouble.
PROVERBS 15:16 NKJV

The greatest treasure does not compare to a life with the Lord either now or eternally. We enter this life with nothing, and we leave with nothing, so we should invest in things eternal rather than things temporal. The path through life goes up and down, but the path that leads into the next life is more important.

We can lean into our eternal futures right now. It starts with the fear of the Lord. Once we lean into knowing God and understanding how awesome he is, and how fearsome he is to the enemy, all pieces of life will line up. When God is first in our lives, a righteous reshuffling occurs that we can trust, love, and live. It's that straightforward.

Lord, following you is not easy, but the path is clear. It's not simple, but it is worthy. Keep my eyes on you.

Eat Vegetables

It is better to eat vegetables with those who love you
than to eat meat with those who hate you.

PROVERBS 15:17 NCV

It's funny to think that people were also avoiding vegetables back in Solomon's day. Despite knowing that vegetables are good for us, the problem persists today. What is Solomon saying here? Vegetables are seen as less desirable than meat, and Solomon is telling us to sacrifice a bit.

It's better to have less and be with those we love rather than indulge ourselves and be subjected to those who hate us. In the same way, it's better to have less in this lifetime to be with God later. God wants us to embrace a basic, simple, or even bland life now to be with him eternally. If we feast on rich, tasty meals in this life, we might end up spending eternity with the one who hates us.

Teach me to embrace a simple life, Lord, if that is what you give me. Give me an eternal perspective so I can focus on what is important.

Quiet Contention

A hot-tempered man stirs up strife,
but he who is slow to anger quiets contention.
PROVERBS 15:18 ESV

It's not pleasant to be in the company of someone who sparks a bad temper with the smallest provocation. Believers are instructed to keep an even temper and to think before responding, especially before reacting to people who create conflict or look for arguments. May we be actors and not reactors.

We can seek specific behaviors to cultivate even tempers. We can contemplate the words spoken and understand the tone of voice. We can consider the motivation of the speaker. We can seek to know the background of a situation. We can pause to see if there is more of the story to be revealed. All these options offer a path through a bad situation and a way to emulate Jesus.

Father, let me speak your Word and your ways. Keep my mouth from sin and give me a way through hot-tempered moments by contemplating words, considering motivations, seeking more information, and pausing in the moment.

The Highway

The way of the lazy man is like a hedge of thorns,
But the way of the upright is a highway.
PROVERBS 15:19 NKJV

A hedge of thorns is a wall in the way. It's a reason to not go forward. It's a reason to stop and do nothing. It's also an excuse for a lazy person to not pursue the Lord. Life with God is a purposeful life. There aren't shortcuts to knowing God and his will; it takes effort.

The highway of the upright is paved with the Word of God. It's protected and preserved with prayer. We have an open invitation to take this highway. God opens his Word for us, and it is full of the love, beauty, and grace of the Almighty Creator. When we choose the way of the upright, he clears the way and makes the road smooth. God loves us, and he wants us to find him when we seek him.

Keep me on the highway to heaven, Father. Keep me close to you and within the freedom of your will.

Sensible and Foolish

Sensible children bring joy to their father;
foolish children despise their mother.
PROVERBS 15:20 NLT

The Lord guides us through the work of the Holy Spirit in our hearts and minds. With him, the paths of our lives change. The more we seek the Word and truth, the more sensible we become. Common sense and holy sense become part of our thinking. We plan and act in submission to God and his will. Everything starts to make spiritual sense. We become better than ourselves because the Holy Spirit dwells in us and directs us with wisdom. This brings joy to our Father.

Rejection of the Father brings him grief. When we plan alone, when we use only the sense we have in our hearts and minds, we are rejecting the higher knowledge of God. Moving through life without consideration of God's plan, making our way without acknowledging our Creator, is foolish. We are putting ourselves higher than God, and it is purposeful marginalization of the Father.

Lord, keep me humble and conscious of your place over my life and within my heart and mind.

The highway of the upright
is to depart from evil;
He who keeps his way
preserves his soul.

PROVERBS 16:17 NKJV

Do Right

A person without wisdom enjoys being foolish,
but someone with understanding does what is right.
PROVERBS 15:21 NCV

Believers often tire of being ridiculed and discredited by others. It's discouraging to see people who don't put God first having a good time and indulging themselves while we live with less as a direct result of doing the right thing. It's difficult to keep our eyes on Jesus when we're living in the world.

The only way to keep our hearts and minds in the right place is to keep close to the Word and pray for the Lord to stay obvious in our lives. We need God, and the most precious result of belonging to him is being with him forever. We need the understanding that goes with God's truth to persist and believe throughout this worldly path. We can watch the foolish enjoying the moment but rest in the wisdom that what is coming to us is far greater.

I love you, Father, and I love your wisdom and understanding. Give me persistence to stay in your Word and pray without ceasing.

Consultation

Without consultation, plans are frustrated,
But with many counselors they succeed.
PROVERBS 15:22 NASB

Do you listen to the input of trusted friends and family before making important plans? Are you in a position to share your strengths and perspectives with others in a respectful way? God is the only omniscient one, so we need each other. He doesn't need to consult anyone before enacting his plans, but we do. Our perspective is limited, so asking others for their help and opinions is crucial for success.

Let's not allow arrogance to come between us and the accomplishment of our plans; we will only be left frustrated if we do. Instead, let's offer help, work together, love each other, find ways to help others succeed, and give God all the credit.

God, in your wisdom and according to your perfect plan, you created each of us differently so we would work better together than on our own. Please set good counselors in my path and show me where to offer my help.

A Timely Word

*A person finds joy in giving an apt reply
and how good is a timely word!*
Proverbs 15:23 NIV

Has someone ever spoken a wise word to you just when you needed it, and it was so fitting you knew it had to be the hand of God at work in that person? This sort of wisdom is not found in a sudden burst of inspiration or breakthrough; it means walking alongside God, hand in hand, and listening to the prompting of the Holy Spirit.

There is joy in being used by God to bless others, and it is always according to his perfect timing. As we spend time with God and fill our hearts with him, we will feel his nudging and be able to offer a timely word of encouragement (or warning) precisely when someone needs it. Often God's chosen method for accomplishing his will is to use us, his children, when we submit ourselves to him.

The answers to all problems are found in you, God. Please hold my hand as I walk through life and use me to encourage others along the way.

Life Winds Upward

The way of life winds upward for the wise,
That he may turn away from hell below.
PROVERBS 15:24 NKJV

Hell is not a joke; it's the default path for each of us if we reject God. The downward trail into the abyss doesn't take effort. It's where we go when we put ourselves first, seek our pleasures, and take the wide road everyone else is taking.

The way of the Lord is narrow and leads uphill. It takes work and focus. It's purposeful and chosen. Believers find amazing blessings on that upward trail, but there's no minimizing the effort required. We need to be "casting down arguments and every high thing that exalts itself against the knowledge of God, bringing every thought into captivity to the obedience of Christ" as Paul writes in 2 Corinthians 10:5. This isn't a passive occurrence. A believer trains their mind and heart to submit to God for the glory that awaits in heaven.

God, I love your upward way of life. I love where you take me and how blessed I am to know you. Keep my faith strong in you.

Gracious Words

The thoughts of the wicked are an abomination to the Lord,
but gracious words are pure.
Proverbs 15:26 ESV

When the Holy Spirit dwells in us, he links us directly to God. He alerts us when we mess up. He teaches us to watch our words. He directs us to think purposefully on goodness and light. God infuses us with holy sensibilities which are higher than common ones. We are one with God and his eternal purpose.

Without the Holy Spirit, we live a random life of self-fulfillment. There is no higher glory to watching our thoughts and words without God. There is no direction for eternal purposes when we live for ourselves. We are on a spiraling, downward path, and our thoughts will demonstrate this. Foolish words and choices characterize people who don't know God, and it's coupled with misplaced definitions of success and worthiness as well.

My Lord, you are worthy of everything gracious and pure. Direct my thoughts and words so they reflect a pure heart.

Greed Brings Grief

Greed brings grief to the whole family,
but those who hate bribes will live.
PROVERBS 15:27 NLT

None of us live in a bubble. What we do and how we think affects everyone around us. We are not victims of our environment. Nature and nurture do play a big part in how we think, but once we repent, our hearts belong to the Lord. We start to see his presence in our lives as we allow the Holy Spirit to do his work. We can submit because the Holy Spirit guides us to that submission.

When we open our hearts to the Holy Spirit, our family and friends are immediately affected. We will speak in an intentional and kinder way. We will pause for the Spirit's feedback and be vessels for the Word. As the Spirit moves through us, our homes will reflect a better light and a holier foundation. The Lord doesn't promise life will get easier—it will likely be harder—but our perspective changes the path, and God's righteousness touches the paths of everyone around us.

Lord, allow me to be a vessel for you within my family. Even if they are not followers of you, I know you can use me to shine your light into their lives.

Righteous Hearts

The heart of the righteous studies how to answer,
But the mouth of the wicked pours forth evil.
Proverbs 15:28 NKJV

The Holy Spirit often pauses our speech so he can have a voice in our responses. Much can be done when we allow the Lord to speak through us. As our hearts submit to him, we can marvel at the divinely inspired words that come out of our mouths. The Holy Spirit's voice brings glory into the moment when we had no capability to do so.

The presence of God in our hearts is life changing. The surge of righteousness is amazing to witness because God's presence is both gentle and a force to be reckoned with. We walk through conversations and situations differently when the Holy Spirit directs our words. Every time we recognize his work in us, let us remember to give glory to him who blesses us in this way.

Thank you, Father, for your presence in my heart. I see how you change situations into blessings for everyone instead of messes. Please speak through me.

The Unheard Wicked

The Lord does not listen to the wicked,
but he hears the prayers of those who do right.
Proverbs 15:29 NCV

Dear believers, we have the ear of God! He listens to us and hears our prayers. It means so much to him when we are focused on him and asking for his directions. If we intentionally look to God for direction, love, grace, or anything we need in the moment, he is there. Sometimes his answer is immediate. Sometimes we need to wait for an answer, but that is God directing us toward growth, patience, or both.

Unbelievers may pray, maybe in a moment of grief or pain, but the Lord will not hear those prayers unless they give him their hearts and souls first. The difference is everything. Either we belong to God, or we don't. If we don't, we are on our own. We don't have the power of the universe in our court, and we don't have God's ear.

Lord, thank you for listening. Thank you for your direction, grace, and love. Thank you for hearing me when you have the whole of creation needing you.

Life-giving Reproof

If you listen to constructive criticism,
you will be at home among the wise.
If you reject discipline, you only harm yourself.
PROVERBS 15:31-32 NLT

Criticism may feel cruel, but it's an opportunity for growth. Why is it so difficult to receive? It may be because accepting criticism means admitting we have flaws and need help. If we want to be "at home among the wise" and not harm ourselves, we need to stay humble enough to receive discipline.

Through discipline, we develop healthy habits; through criticism, we can learn and grow. Accepting both measures will help us move on from our pasts and improve. If we want to become more like Christ, we must learn to embrace loving correction.

Lord, your reproof is life-giving, and I accept it. I pray for wisdom to make the most of the opportunities criticism and correction offer me so I may mature into who you want to be and glorify you in the process.

Kind Correction

If you listen to correction, you grow in understanding.
PROVERBS 15:32 NLT

It does not feel good to have our shortcomings pointed out and addressed, but praise God for the person who cares enough to do so! Let's recognize this as the loving gift that it is and learn from any truth spoken. This is the process of maturing.

We can also offer loving correction to those who need it and are wise enough to listen. Knowing how difficult it is to receive correction, try to deliver it in love and godliness. The point of correction should always be growth and understanding and never to put someone else down or puff ourselves up. Self-advancing criticism is nether caring nor honoring to God. Any correction ought to be helpful, not harmful, to the other person. When someone else corrects us, let's be hungry to learn and mature, our ears are open to any truth and graciously disregarding anything that does not align with God's reproof. Then we are sure to become more like Christ.

Jesus, give me a heart like yours both to receive and deliver correction. My goal in both is a better understanding of you.

Humility Precedes Honor

Fear of the Lord teaches wisdom;
humility precedes honor.
Proverbs 15:33 NLT

There's a process to acquiring wisdom. The Lord knows the best way for us to learn, and he knows what we can absorb and when. When we lean into him and concern ourselves with his processes, the blessing is a righteous path.

We begin with humility. It isn't inherent in the human spirit to be humble. We tend to justify ourselves and defend our choices, but those reactions don't open the door to understanding and humility. Once we assume our unworthiness, we then assume God's worthiness. We start to hear his voice, and things change. Our words have more intention and honesty. We reflect more on the larger meaning of what is going on. We have eyes that see and hearts that move with the compassion of the Holy Spirit dwelling in us. That's when wisdom gets a foothold.

Lord, let me see wisdom. Keep my heart in check with humility and put me on a path that will lead to an honorable character and a wise insight.

Commit to the Lord

Commit your work to the Lord,
and your plans will be established.
Proverbs 16:3 ESV

When something is established, it is already successful. It has already been arranged and the plans put into motion. Although we can't always see where the path of faith is leading, we can be certain that God's plans are good and cannot be undone.

True success can only be found when we are rooted and established in God. When we read his Word, learn his heart, and follow his ways, nothing and no one can thwart the good plans he has in store for us. They have already been established! The deed is signed.

I commit everything I do to you, dear Lord. I place in your hand all that concerns me and all my plans for the future. Please take my aspirations, hopes, and dreams and mold them to match yours. You are committed to me, I am committed to you, and nothing can come between us.

On Purpose

The LORD has made everything for its purpose,
even the wicked for the day of trouble.
PROVERBS 16:4 ESV

God does not make mistakes. God created you! You are designed, intentional, and made with a purpose in mind. Whatever decisions are confronting you today, remember who you are and whose you are. Commit your decisions to God because he is trustworthy and good. Trust him with the outcome because he is faithful and wise.

Everything has a purpose, so even if it doesn't make sense to you today, rest assured that your loving Father has it under control. You do not need to worry about a future God has already written. You do not need to live as anything less than the masterpiece he lovingly designed.

Lord, you have a purpose for everything you have created, and that includes me. I find fulfillment in this purpose even when it is unpleasant or painful. I will find my purpose in you and strive to be faithful to your calling.

The Lord Directs

A man's heart plans his way,
But the L*ORD directs his steps.*
PROVERBS 16:9 NKJV

When was the last time you asked for God's blessing on your schedule? Do you pray over your calendar? Are you emotionally open to God intervening and switching things around? Is the first thing you think about in the morning the King who created you, or is it your daily to-do list?

We make all sorts of plans, but we can't take a single step without the grace of God guiding us forward. God paves our paths, God can turn our stress into joy, and God holds the future in his hands. When we make our plans, we can consider what God may be saying to us. Let's never forget to factor in the most important things. Nothing happens apart from God, so instead of wrestling with him, let's align with him and trust him with the unknown.

Everything I do is for your glory, dear God. Please take my agenda and make it what you want. Keep me flexible and reverent before you. Your ways are greater than my ways, and I choose to follow you.

Watch Your Actions

Good people stay away from evil.
By watching what they do, they protect their lives.
Proverbs 16:17 NCV

It's often not difficult to find a response to events and people. We are full of feelings and opinions. What requires insight and effort is crafting a response that holds goodness and mercy. That kind of response isn't always easy or intuitive. Most humanity veers toward negativity and criticism.

Christians, however, are instructed to love God and others. We have the most incredible example: the sacrificial love of Jesus Christ. When Jesus died on the cross after being beaten and abused for the sake of every sin across time, he went through a horrific death. He spent three days in the pit so we would never have to go there. He loved us first, and now we can love others rather than partake in the evil in this world. We are assured of our futures; we know where we're going. It is loving to show others the path of Jesus.

Father, I love your presence and power in my life, and I want you to show me how to lead others into your love.

Pride Before Destruction

Pride goes before destruction,
and a haughty spirit before a fall.
PROVERBS 16:18 ESV

Haughtiness isn't a nice look on a person's face. It twists what could be pleasant into contempt and disregard. A proud spirit shows in a person's demeanor. It mangles the lovely and forfeits goodness. The effects of these heart-level attitudes don't only show on the surface. Pride and a haughty spirit reveal the innermost intentions, and they have a direct effect on a person's outcome.

In daily life, a proud person will, at some point, be humbled. A person looking contemptuously at others will be brought down. If someone lasts a lifetime with these self-centered and harmful attitudes, they fall to eternal destruction. The Word warns us that this is a terrible place, and the only way to avoid it is through the Father's amazing grace.

Dear Father, please reflect your glory through me so I don't walk through life with a contemptuous and prideful heart. Purify me to be as white as snow.

Live Humbly

Better to live humbly with the poor
than to share plunder with the proud.
PROVERBS 16:19 NLT

Throughout the Word, we are taught to store our treasures in heaven and live focused on what matters. Fame, wealth, comfort, and ease are all treasures of this life and don't have any value in eternity. There's a good reason; they are all fueled by selfishness.

When we are fueled by the Holy Spirit, the pursuits of the world and comfort lose their steam. They become less motivating. We are more motivated by the characteristics of our Lord: sacrifice, compassion, understanding, and love. The treasures of a life fueled by these attitudes are of true worth. Other people are brought into the kingdom and lives are transformed because of the work of the Holy Spirit in his people who are willing to put aside selfish pursuits.

Live through me, Holy Spirit. Love through me and allow me to emulate those selfless qualities I don't naturally feel.

Happy to Trust

He who heeds the word wisely will find good,
And whoever trusts in the LORD, happy is he.
PROVERBS 16:20 NKJV

What God says matters. God put every word into Scripture with intentionality. The truth and love contained within those pages are the entire reason we exist. They are not just the goal; they are everything from purpose to path to plan. We will find the whys, the how's, the what's, and the who's in the Word of God.

People who release their self-preserving default and submit to God Almighty start to understand the power now living in them. The love and purpose of God provides all we need to live for him. Wisdom is infused within our hearts and souls, and the glory and wonder we experience because of this is only understood if experienced. We listen to him, and he fills us up. We follow him, and he provides the plan. We submit our hearts, and he gives us otherworldly happiness. That is our purpose.

God, I need your purpose in my life. I need you to provide the power and the plan. Thank you for giving me all the amazing feelings that come with serving you.

Fountain Gives Life

Understanding is like a fountain
which gives life to those who use it,
but foolishness brings punishment to fools.
PROVERBS 16:22 NCV

A fountain splashes and flows from its beautiful height to refresh and relax those around it. It gives life; it reflects light; it calms the soul with its beauty. Solomon says that's what understanding does to those who use it.

Where do we get understanding? From the Holy Spirit as he dwells within our hearts and directs our paths toward heaven. We keep our eyes on God and the Word he has written for us, and we gain understanding. With understanding, we splash beauty and light to others around us. Foolishness is the direct result of not following the directions of the Holy Spirit.

Lord, make me a fountain of understanding. Help me comprehend what your Word says and allow me to bring beauty and light to everyone I know and meet.

Teach My Mouth

The heart of the wise teaches his mouth,
And adds learning to his lips.
PROVERBS 16:23 NKJV

The mouth is a vessel for the heart. Our hearts hold our attitudes and our beliefs about life and other people. Where we invest our time, learning, and relationships crafts the direction our hearts take. We choose where to invest ourselves, and we are blessed with the freedom to do well with our choices or fail.

When we reflect the Holy Spirit dwelling in our hearts, we start to acquire the wisdom God speaks about throughout Scripture but especially in Proverbs. God blessed Solomon with wisdom, not just for his time and place, but also to be recorded in the Word for all time and all people. Wisdom can dwell in every person, and the choice to learn rests with us.

Help me learn, oh God. Speak your wisdom through me and let me be your mouth. Let me know your presence at a heart level so I can live in a way that edifies you.

Powerful Words

Kind words are like honey
sweet to the soul and healthy for the body.
PROVERBS 16:24 NLT

A demoralized person can quickly become a sick person. Many studies examine the physical effect a person's emotional wellbeing has on them. Speaking a kind word to someone can have a positive effect on their physical wellbeing.

Do you speak up when you have a kind word for someone, or do you keep silent? Ask for God's help and boldness in discerning when a kind word should be spoken. When someone knows they're appreciated or accepted, they are less likely to be anxious. When someone knows they're loved, they tend to be less worried. A word spoken in love can bring someone's defenses down and cool their anger. Both kind and cruel words are powerful, and both tend to spread like wildfire. Choose which fire you start with the words you use.

Words hold power, and I want to use my words to glorify you, God. I will speak words of life and bring healing to those around me. Please keep my heart pure and my tongue kind.

See the Signs

Whoever winks his eyes plans dishonest things;
he who purses his lips brings evil to pass.
PROVERBS 16:30 ESV

Believers need discernment to grasp the blessing of wisdom. Discernment separates the thorn from the rose and discards it so it can't harm others. People who purposefully plan dishonesty can be found out by the Holy Spirit, and Christians can follow the Spirit to avoid evil and help others see it as well. Without the Holy Spirit, we are at the mercy of our understanding and an unfiltered view of the circumstances.

When we live in the power of the Almighty, we work for the eternal kingdom. This provides us with the purpose of revealing the evil one's intentions to ourselves and others. We are infused with truth and love, and that power is capable and desirous of good. We have a way through dishonest plans and evil intentions with amazing love and infallible discernment.

God Almighty, I bow down to you. I submit my heart, head, and mouth to do your work. Help me understand what is going on in the heavenly realms. Help me work for your kingdom.

Crown of Gray

Gray hair is like a crown of honor;
it is earned by living a good life.
PROVERBS 16:31 NCV

Our culture discredits age unnecessarily and unfairly. The Bible tells us a good life earns us honor in old age. There will always be fools at any age, but those who have spent their lives listening to the voice of God and learning his Word have also learned wisdom, and with wisdom comes honor.

Giving respect to older believers opens doors to experiences and opportunities we would otherwise not know about. We ourselves show wisdom when we respect and honor the people who did so much before we got here. The Lord promises to lengthen the days of some believers, and this helps younger ones hear the stories and grow in glory through older saints.

Open my eyes and ears, Lord, so I can hear the wisdom of the saints who have done your work for many years more than I have. Let me humbly approach your kingdom with a thirst for knowing you and the stories of your people.

Better than Mighty

One who is slow to anger is better than the mighty,
And one who rules his spirit, than one who captures a city.
PROVERBS 16:32 NASB

Before we can control our circumstances, we need to learn how to control ourselves. Left undisturbed, most of us are decent and kind people, but how do we respond when someone or something disrupts us? How do we handle being treated unfairly? When our sense of control is threatened, do we exercise self-control, or do we lash out? Being slow to anger is more impressive than brute strength. It is more difficult to rule our impulses than it is to rule a city.

Self-control is a sign of wisdom and maturity. It demonstrates our reliance on God to control what we cannot. It offers safety and stability to our loved ones, and it's a leadership quality others will notice and learn from. Let's practice ruling our spirits every day until we have learned to control our reactions.

God, help me control my spirit so I am not subject to impulsive feelings. Instead of lashing out, teach me to be patient and long-suffering. I want to keep my sinful nature in check and rely on you for guidance.

Forgiveness

Love overlooks the mistakes of others,
but dwelling on the failures of others devastates friendships.
PROVERBS 17:9 TPT

How can we forgive someone who hasn't asked to be forgiven? It starts with recognizing who forgiveness is between. The offender may be blessed and relieved by receiving forgiveness, but forgiveness starts between our hearts and the heart of God.

God forgave us for every evil thing we do, and he expects us to also forgive others; not because they deserve it, but because we were also undeserving. Forgiving others means healing our hearts from the pain we're carrying. It means laying it at the feet of Jesus and letting it go. Forgiving others does not mean we trust someone who is untrustworthy or place ourselves in a position to be hurt again, but it does mean our hurt and offense no longer resides in us or has power over us. It's finished. It's forgiven.

Dear Lord, make me a person of integrity who is worthy of the gifts you give. I want to be worthy of your name and the calling you have placed on my life. I don't deserve your love, but I accept it and thank you for it.

Keep Peace

Don't be one who is quick to quarrel,
for an argument is hard to stop,
and you never know how it will end,
so don't even start down that road!
PROVERBS 17:14 TPT

As children of God, it is important to work for peace and refuse to let anger get the best of us. We must keep our egos in check and make sure we're living to glorify God. This may mean apologizing first or refusing to engage in a meaningless argument.

God doesn't want us to live frustrated or combative lives. An argument can quickly spin out of control when anger is steering, so it's better to stay calm and refuse to continue when the disagreement no longer holds hope of growth and maturity. The more anger it draws out, the faster it grows. Soon it controls us instead of us controlling it. Children of God are supposed to be people of peace. That's an easy calling when everyone is getting along, but it's vitally important when it's difficult.

Prince of Peace, when someone comes at me in an argumentative way, help me rise above anger and diffuse the situation. Words are like fire, and I want to bring calm, to the situation.

True Friendship

A friend loves at all times,
and a brother is born for a time of adversity.
PROVERBS 17:17 NIV

Tough times bond people closely. Have you had difficult days which produced mature friendships? Often rough roads reveal your real friends. God promises to be with us in good and bad times, and that's the kind of friendship we should also emulate.

Bad days are part of life. When a friend is going through something difficult, let's put our agendas aside, remember we're all part of God's family, and be there for them when they need it most. Adversity should not scare us away from being a good friend just like Jesus is for us.

Father God, thank you for the friends you have given me who stand with me through thick and thin. Above all, thank you for your friendship.

Judge Wisely

It's poor judgment to guarantee another person's debt or put up security for a friend.

PROVERBS 17:18 NLT

Once money gets involved in any relationship, things change. The Lord structured the family to be a safe place for money to exist, and there are governmental and corporate laws in place for the interchanging of money to be legal and safe. There are good reasons for God to tell us not to get involved with anyone else's debt.

There are ways to be kind to our friends with money. We can give them a gift. We can intervene with other services like providing meals, childcare, or housekeeping. This can free up more time for our friends to earn the money to repay their debt. If asked and if we are qualified, we can provide some advice. There are many ways to help people without assuming responsibility for their debts.

Lord, allow me to discern wisely when people, especially friends, ask me for help. Let me be generous in ways that make sense and honor you.

Word Restraint

*The one who has knowledge uses words with restraint,
and whoever has understanding is even-tempered.*
PROVERBS 17:27 NIV

Every believer hopes to be the person who controls their tongue and temper. It is an admirable quality to be able to rein in inappropriate speech and misplaced anger. What if we could only say things that respect God and feel angry only about things God is angry about? That would be perfection.

But we're not perfect. We're products of a fallen world. Sin swirls around us constantly, but that's where we meet God. We can't follow the Lord's way if we don't need him to gain control of our sinful nature. We can't understand a healthy dependency on God, nor the love and grace he has for us, if we don't first understand our need for him. When we fail, we get back up, ask for forgiveness, receive grace, and are redeemed. It's a beautiful dance as we get closer and closer to knowing our precious Redeemer.

Lord, each time I miss the mark, let me know. Please accept my repentance again and again and as many times as it takes for me to know you better.

Calamity and Crookedness

A man of crooked heart does not discover good,
and one with a dishonest tongue falls into calamity.
PROVERBS 17:20 ESV

It doesn't take long to see the hearts of the people around us. The fruit is there for all to see. We must be willing to acknowledge what we observe and be honest about it. Hope doesn't have to die when we only see no good and constant calamity. Hope starts in bad places where the Lord can shine his light and chase out darkness.

We start in dark places. The reason we know Jesus is because we reached a moment when we knew we needed him. Every sinner begins the path to redemption in the dark, so we need to pray for the crooked heart and the dishonest tongue even if that evil is leveled against us. We will spend eternity with the King, and those poor souls don't know the light of his kingdom yet.

Thank you, God, for being good. I discover every good thing when I discover you.

October
Wisdom is the principal thing;
Therefore get wisdom.
And in all your getting, get understanding.
Proverbs 4:7 NKJV

Joyful Heart

A joyful, cheerful heart brings healing
to both body and soul.
But the one whose heart is crushed
struggles with sickness and depression.
PROVERBS 17:22 TPT

God wants the best for us, so he offers us his joy. His joy is greater than our situations and problems because it points us toward an eternity with him. It puts our temporary trials into proper perspective. Still, we need to nourish and care for both our bodies and souls. It is not more spiritual to ignore our physical wellbeing; he created our bodies to house our souls.

When Elijah was depressed and cried out that he wanted to die, God answered by having him take a nap and sending an angel to bake bread. See 1 Kings 19:4-6. Our loving Creator knows we're physical and spiritual beings, and he cares for our physical and spiritual needs. One way he does this is by filling us with his joy. Ask him for that today.

Your joy is nothing like what the world offers, dear Lord. It surpasses physical conditions and goes beyond circumstances. Please fill my heart with your everlasting joy so I can never be crushed.

Fools Wander

The person with understanding
is always looking for wisdom,
but the mind of a fool wanders everywhere.
PROVERBS 17:24 NCV

When the Lord directs our paths, we have true direction. Sometimes, especially during transitional times, the view of the path is only about an inch in front of the big toe. When we graduate from school, get married, have a baby, find a new job, retire: all these seasons are critical for dependency on God. When we lean into his wisdom, he gives it to us. We see the next step, gain clarity on issues, and can move ahead with confidence.

When we depend on only ourselves and whatever knowledge we possess in the moment, we aren't tapping into the greatest intelligence and wisdom in existence. We're caught in this place and time, and that's the extent of our resources. It's very limiting, and according to Scripture, it makes us foolish. Wisdom is knowing and relying on the source of wisdom itself: the Almighty.

Father, keep me in your heart and within your sights whenever I have another decision to make. May I always seek your face for true wisdom.

Bitterness and Grief

Foolish children bring grief to their father
and bitterness to the one who gave them birth.
PROVERBS 17:25 NLT

Grief and sadness engulf a parent when they see their child choosing to discount experiences and life lessons. It is painful to watch a child walk away from God, eternity, family, love, and healthy relationships. It is also one of the best reasons to spend buckets of time with the Lord in prayer.

Imagine the grief God must feel on our behalf when we, his beloved creation, choose to reject his love and live foolishly. Let's be wise, reject foolishness, and return again and again to God. We can pray for those wavering or wandering, even those who have rejected the truth, so they might return to their awaiting Creator. Give everything to the Lord. Some people seem terminally lost, but that is not for us to decide. Prayer is critical, and love is the guide.

Lord, help me love the people in my family no matter what. Teach me to be like you for their sake and to keep coming back to you in my grief and pain.

Beaten Leaders

It is not good to punish the innocent
or to beat leaders for being honest.
PROVERBS 17:26 NCV

It's nonsensical to punish people who are innocent or honest, but we know history proves this can happen all too easily. When perceptions become more trusted than facts, we must rely even more on God. God is the origin of truth. He is the Creator of goodness, and he ordained our salvation in love.

Throughout time, there are more tribulations for people than there are easy times. It is critical to understand that all things are for God's glory. Our tasks revolve around seeking the Lord and doing his will as best we can. There will be innocent people punished and honest leaders beaten, but we live to help any who are persecuted when they are within our reach. May we reach as many as possible for God's glory.

Let me be a light, Father, for those who are unjustly punished or persecuted. May I see where I can help and move quickly to serve.

Even-Tempered

The one who has knowledge uses words with restraint,
and whoever has understanding is even-tempered.
PROVERBS 17:27 NIV

It is a miracle to witness, within us or others, how the Lord changes us once we follow and seek him. Behavior is corrected and speech is edifying. Love motivates us. Sincere care and concern emulate from God's people as they become vessels of his love.

Salvation gives us an awareness of how we speak and act and the impact we have on other people. We begin to care about God's love shining through us to others. Our words show restraint because the gospel will strike the hearts of sinners if distractions don't get in the way. Reactions from unbelievers will vary, but when believers show even tempers, God's message has an avenue to travel for the good of his kingdom.

Lord, make me more like you. Give me your wise and caring character and let your words flow from my mouth.

Silence Seems Wise

Even a fool who keeps silent is considered wise;
when he closes his lips, he is deemed intelligent.
PROVERBS 17:28 ESV

It is worthwhile learning how to listen. To reach people for Jesus, we need to understand their hearts. It doesn't change the message, but it may alter the speed of delivery, or the path chosen to speak about our Redeemer. If an unbeliever chooses to stay quiet, it is important to meet that silence with compassion and a willingness to listen. It's equally important to not mistake the silence for faith.

A lot can go on in a person's heart without revealing much before we get to know them well, but the effort to befriend someone is never for naught. At the very least, they know we care. That matters sometimes more than we know. Trust the Lord; trust him when he works through believers. When an unbeliever speaks, keep in mind that the fount of all wisdom and intelligence has not yet taken root in their heart.

Lord, may I be your vessel for truth and wisdom, and may I never become arrogant. I am the clay, and you are the potter.

Better Together

Whoever isolates himself seeks his own desire;
he breaks out against all sound judgment.
PROVERBS 18:1 ESV

Isolation produces questionable judgment. Doing life with other people is challenging, but it's healthy and necessary. Being vulnerable with others keeps us accountable and honest. We can't stray off God's path when we walk hand in hand with wise and committed brothers and sisters.

The importance of community cannot be overstated. Relationships are a gift from God to be treasured and fought for. Working through disagreements teaches us to care for others and set aside our pride. In the moment, it may seem easier to withdraw from the work of relationships, but in the end, it is harder because none of us were meant to walk alone.

Lord, please remind me to prioritize fellowship with other believers so I don't wander astray, or have my faith grow cold. I want to surround myself with positive, godly influences.

A Brother Offended

A brother who has been insulted
is harder to win back than a walled city,
and arguments separate people
like the barred gates of a palace.
PROVERBS 18:19 NCV

Insults can be stronger than a fortified city. Once an emotional wall is put up, it's challenging to bring the relationship back to a place of trust and vulnerability. As ambassadors of Christ, it is important we think before we speak, avoid foolish talk, and use wise words.

The closer we are to someone, the deeper the insult may run if we hurt them. We care about the opinions of those we are closest and most intimate with, so let's be especially loving and honoring within our closest relationships. It's easier to work on being kind at the forefront than it is to repair a wound already inflicted.

God, I don't want to hurt anyone, but sometimes offense occurs. Please teach me to speak wisely, forgive completely, and fight for the relationships worth fighting for. Keep me humble and kind and please broaden my perspective so I can better consider the feelings of others.

A Fruitful Harvest

From the fruit of their mouth a person's stomach is filled; with the harvest of their lips they are satisfied.
PROVERBS 18:20 NIV

Short of medical intervention, nothing reaches the belly without first going through the mouth. Today's verse speaks about the fruit of the mouth, and it offers a quick leap to the fruit of the Spirit. To recap, Galatians 5:22-23 outlines the fruit of the Spirit as love, joy, peace, patience, kindness, goodness, faithfulness, gentleness, and self-control. Every one of these qualities can come from the mouth.

We speak out of our hearts; our mouths are just the vehicles. When we emulate the Holy Spirit, we mull on the ways we have changed from who we previously were. When our hearts are infused with the fruit of the Spirit, thanks to the Spirit working in us, we feel fulfilled; we are satisfied. We gratefully give more control to him as we learn to trust him with every detail of our lives.

Holy Spirit, I welcome your presence in my heart. I am grateful for the work you are doing to make me into a closer reflection of Jesus.

Spoken Word

Your words are so powerful
that they will kill or give life.
PROVERBS 18:21 TPT

How is it possible that what we say can bring forth life or death? Well, there are extreme examples: the person bullied into committing suicide, or the person who talked the suicidal person off the ledge. In our daily lives, however, how is this verse applicable?

Words hold a lot of power. God's written Word gives us life; the devil's wicked whisperings bring destruction and death. When we speak, it reflects what is in our hearts and spreads that message to others. What message have we hidden in our hearts: God's or the devil's? Whose words are we spreading? Both God and the devil have plans for our lives and the lives of those we impact. Let's refuse to complain, gossip, slander others, or be insulting with our words. Our words can further the plan of God which leads to life.

Lord, make me aware of the power of my words. Please fill my heart with love and joy so it pours from my mouth. Teach me to be measured and tempered in all the words I speak.

Poor Versus Rich

The poor use entreaties,
but the rich answer roughly.
PROVERBS 18:23 ESV

So much of our time and energy is spent trying to change the behavior, decisions, or paths of other people. The two methods in today's verse give us insight into a heart's motivation. People who are poor have few resources and often little confidence from either failures or a lack of positive results for their efforts. Rich people have loads of confidence but little patience, so they don't always concern themselves with the impact their words are having on others. Both methods of getting changes lack one thing: God.

God doesn't beg or speak roughly. God stands righteously above the circumstances we find ourselves in, and he offers us a beautiful eternity by the repentance of our sins in the sacrificial blood of Christ, and that's it. It's clear and concise. Take it or leave it without coercion or force. God wants each one of us to accept his love and grace, but he won't beg, and he won't force us.

Thank you, God, for your beautiful ways. Thank you for coming into my life and speaking to me with so much love and respect that there's no room for coercion or aggression. I love you deeply.

Friend of God

One who has unreliable friends soon comes to ruin,
but there is a friend who sticks closer than a brother.
PROVERBS 18:24 NIV

We are blessed to have friends, and we have faced sticky situations with some of them. In everything, Jesus says he's our friend, and he has set a perfect example of what true friendship looks like. He never leaves us even when the days grow dark, and times are tough. He does not use us for his own gain but instead left his throne in heaven to come and save us.

He truly loves us for who we are and not who we could be. He's not interested in our wealth or fame; he wants a relationship. He cares about what we care about even if it's unimportant. If it's important to us, then it's important to him. He is patient, caring, understanding, and always nearby when we need him. He is the perfect friend. Let's learn from his example and be good friends too.

Jesus, thank you for being my friend. Thank you for giving me other friends and for teaching me how to be a friend. Friendship is valuable, and I don't take it for granted.

Do Yourself a Favor

Those who get wisdom do themselves a favor,
and those who love learning will succeed.
PROVERBS 19:8 NCV

Are you succeeding at life? What does that even mean? What would you measure on a scale of poor to rich? Failure to fame? Detestable to holy? Well, how does the Lord measure success? Consider Jesus' words in Matthew 16:26-27, "It is worthless to have the whole world if they lose their souls. They could never pay enough to buy back their souls. The Son of Man will come again with his Father's glory and with his angels. At that time, he will reward them for what they have done."

God does not care about the fame or fortune we accumulate; he doesn't even care about our Good Christian Checklists. He wants us to take what he says to heart and live it out. He wants us to love others honestly and deeply. We need his wisdom to know how to succeed, and we need to spend time with him to obtain it because true wisdom comes only from him.

Your Word, dear God, is rich in teaching. It is packed with wisdom and insight. I want to dig deeper into what you have to say and learn everything I can about your greatness and your plans.

Discretion

A person's insight gives him patience,
and his virtue is to overlook an offense.
PROVERBS 19:11 CSB

Previously, we looked at how difficult it is to rebuild trust and openness in a relationship once insult has erected a wall. Today, let's take the other position and talk about how to stop building those walls. We can't control the actions, feelings, or decisions of others, but we can control our own. Nobody builds our walls for us, and nobody speaks our words.

Offense is an easy snare to fall into because, in some backwards way, it feels good. Do you know what feels better and is healthier and more beneficial? Forgiveness. Self-control. Love. Instead of being quick to anger and offense, let's remember how much grace, patience, and forgiveness God has shown us. That should spur us on to be gracious, patient, and forgiving to others as well.

When I am tempted to be offended, Lord, remind me of the grace you have shown me. If anyone has cause to be offended, it's you, yet you forgive and teach me so I can be better. I want to be that way to other people too. I want to live in love and not offense.

Accepting Correction

Listen to advice and accept discipline,
So that you may be wise the rest of your days.
PROVERBS 19:20 NASB

God uses many methods to teach and nurture us; he speaks to us or nudges our conscience through the Holy Spirit, he gives us his Scripture, and he places wise people around us to offer encouragement and counsel. It is up to us to accept or reject counsel and discipline, but we will be wiser and our lives more blessed if we humbly listen and receive it.

Discipline does not feel good in the moment, but it matures us beyond the point we can achieve alone. We are told in Hebrews 12:6 that God disciplines us because he loves us. The next time you are called to accountability, someone wise offers you correction, or God turns the tables on your plans, instead of rebelling, calm your heart and listen. It is because you are loved and matter to God that these things are happening.

Lord, thank you for your tough love. Thank you for being a caring father who doesn't leave me to my destructive tendencies. Thank you for the people you have put in my life who call me to a higher standard and help me grow.

By Design

A person may have many ideas
concerning God's plan for his life,
but only the designs of God's purpose
will succeed in the end.
PROVERBS 19:21 TPT

Are you a visionary, or do you take more of a backseat to life? Whatever your persona, you probably have some ideas as to how your future will unfold. It's important to plan, but it's even more vital to stay flexible and available to God's interventions. He has a perfect plan in place. Only he has proper perspective and knows what is coming down the road.

Do your plans align with God's plans? What has he laid on your heart to accomplish? If this is a difficult question to answer, imagine what you would spend your time doing if money were not an issue and you knew you wouldn't fail. God has designed you to play an important part. What ideas has God put in your heart, and how are you aligning your life with them today?

God, I want my dreams and ideas to line up with your purposes and plans. Your design for me is ideal. If my plans become too self-centered, please lead me back to your perfect plan.

Loyalty Is Attractive

Loyalty makes a person attractive.
It is better to be poor than dishonest.
PROVERBS 19:22 NLT

Over and over, we see the character of a person matters than physical looks. It's also amazing how our looks are affected by the condition of our hearts: the kindness we show to others, the way we speak, and our loyalty. If we show up for our friends, that means something. If we defend people when others speak poorly about them, that can change hearts and increase trust. People who stand up for others in the face of derision or conflict show they are not intimidated by untruthful voices or evil intentions.

At no point does God want us to forfeit integrity. We keep being loyal to others. We don't bend the truth one iota. We face life as a book wide open. There is nothing to hide when you answer to the King of kings. Even when we face poverty, discrimination, or persecution, nothing is worth wavering from the truth and beauty of our loving and graceful God.

Give me strength, oh Father, to say what needs to be said when it needs to be said. Help me not waver in the moment that matters. Help me stay true to you and others.

Good Fear

The fear of the LORD leads to life,
and whoever has it rests satisfied;
he will not be visited by harm.
PROVERBS 19:23 ESV

To fear God is to be awed by him. This type of fear also has a seasoning of actual fear. We don't serve a soft god; we serve a fierce one. He is perfect and pure. He is the beginning and the end. He is all we need, and as we walk this path with him, we learn he is all we want. Everything else we love falls into the box of beautiful blessings that come from serving him, but he is the source of all joy.

There is no satisfaction like fulfilling the purpose for which we were created. When we are saved, we acknowledge God as our Maker. Since he is the Maker of everyone and everything, he is equipped to fully know each one of us. He has a plan, and we are fulfilled as we live out that plan. We find our reasons for being and we become the best of ourselves in every way. Because we are also destined for eternity, we can never be snatched away from our Lord.

Dear Lord, lead me in your way and teach me to rest in the plan you have made for me.

Food Not Eaten

Lazy people take food in their hand
but don't even lift it to their mouth.
PROVERBS 19:24 NIV

People will hear the gospel; they will go to church or know believers. The most shocking thing about the truth of Jesus Christ is that so many people will be handed it but won't take it. They hear the Word, and they see lives changed by it. They might acknowledge God is probably in charge of the whole thing, but they don't do anything about it. It isn't worth the effort for them.

It's hard to imagine anything more worthy than serving the Almighty, but this problem is ancient. God walked with Adam and Eve and talked with them in the Garden of Eden, yet they distrusted and disbelieved. Of their first two sons, Cain and Abel, one trusted God and the other killed his brother. "Taste and see that the Lord is good; blessed is the one who takes refuge in him," are David's words in Psalm 34:8. Trusting God requires putting the Word into the mouth and chewing. It takes effort and intention.

Give me your Word, Lord. Show me that my effort is worth everything. Let me be an example of a servant who joyfully makes every effort to reach out to others.

Listen Closely

If you stop listening to instruction, my child,
you will turn your back on knowledge.
PROVERBS 19:27 NLT

We were created to be lifelong learners. We have the Word of God to reference daily, and we praise God for that. Life is a path and not a destination; eternity is the destination. God has structured us to both serve and learn every day. Serving is fueled by learning, and the need to know is fueled by serving. The two belong together.

We can't force knowledge into existence. We need someone to teach us, and there is so much to know in this lifetime that we simply can't know everything. That is by design. God knows everything; we will learn as we need to know, and he crafts us for each special project and purpose he has planned. Joy comes in both the learning and the use of knowledge. We serve his purposes, and he fulfills our dreams.

Father, I belong to you, and I want to serve you all my days. Please teach me and send me the teachers I need so I may fulfill all you have destined for me.

Wine Mocks

Wine is a mocker and beer a brawler;
whoever is led astray by them is not wise.
PROVERBS 20:1 NIV

The effects of alcohol are felt by all of us as a society and by most of us on a personal level. It's no laughing matter when alcohol eats at the existence of a loved one within our families or friend groups. At some point and on some level, this behavior was a choice; then it got out of hand and became an addiction. That's when help is needed to break the chain and release that person back into a healthy life. It's doable and desirable.

Solomon said drunkenness strays from proper behavior. It doesn't bring peaceful relationships; it creates conflict. We get a heightened sense of self-righteousness and self-worth when we imbibe in more wine or beer than our bodies can handle. It leads us astray. Wisdom is avoiding overindulgence. Wisdom is knowing when to stop. Wisdom is stopping before improper behavior is ever experienced.

Lord, you are my Lord and King. I am grateful for your standards and instructions because you are the source of wisdom. Show me when my likes become addictions before it goes too far.

True Friends

Many will say they are loyal friends,
but who can find one who is truly reliable?
The godly walk with integrity;
blessed are their children who follow them.

PROVERBS 20:6-7 NLT

True friends show each other respect, and they aren't turned away by petty grievances. Loyal friends want the best for each other and don't leave when life gets tough. There's an old African proverb that says, "If you want to go fast, go alone. If you want to go far, go together."

God did not design us to walk through life alone, so take time to slow down and help your friends. If you need help, reach out, ask for it, and find out who your loyal friends are. Jesus showed us through his own life what it means to be a true friend, so let's follow his example. Truly loyal friends are rare, so hold on to them and be one yourself.

Lord, teach me to walk with integrity and be a loyal friend. I want to be someone my friends can trust and count on to be there for them. Thank you for being my friend and giving me friends I can turn to.

Work for Wealth

Wealth inherited quickly in the beginning
will do you no good in the end.
PROVERBS 20:21 NCV

Having wealth handed to us might be a dream, but it will not do us any good in the end. Paul wrote to the Ephesians about the God-given need we have to work. "God has made us what we are. In Christ Jesus, God made us to do good works, which God planned in advance for us to live our lives doing," according to Ephesians 2:10. The essence of work didn't start with people; it started with God.

After working for six days to create all we know and love, God rested. We read in Genesis 2:2, "By the seventh day God finished the work he had been doing, so he rested from all his work." Since we are created in his image, and the first activity we know God did was work, it's logical to assume we will be happy and fulfilled behaving as our Maker did. We need work to be most like God. We need to work to provide for our generation and to teach the next generation how to work and provide for their generation.

Thank you, Father, for the work you planned for me in advance. I am grateful to know work can bring me closer to you since you also work.

Give Way

Don't say, "I will get even for this wrong."
Wait for the LORD to handle the matter.
PROVERBS 20:22 NLT

In the moment of attack or persecution, it is superhuman to not retaliate. How do we not slap the person who slaps us? Retaliation is human, and that is why Jesus instructs us to be superhuman; it requires us to depend on him. "You have heard the law that says the punishment must match the injury: 'An eye for an eye, and a tooth for a tooth.' But I say, do not resist an evil person! If someone slaps you on the right cheek, offer the other cheek also" (Matthew 5:38-39).

It takes work to let offenses go. It takes superhuman work to do so. It helps, however, to remind ourselves of how much we have been forgiven and focus on God's saving grace. If we think about all our sins and the redemption we received the moment we repented, it is easier to let go of the offenses others hurl at us.

Keep me holy, Lord. I am unworthy, but I love you, and you are always worthy. By your blood and your resurrection, I am saved from my sin. Teach me to let go of offense.

Dishonest Scales

The LORD detests double standards;
he is not pleased by dishonest scales.
PROVERBS 20:23 NLT

It's arguably harder today to skew a scale than it was in biblical times, but we are more creative in our efforts to cheat and steal. The problem hasn't gone away; it's simply different. The point is the same: God hates double standards and dishonesty.

Integrity is a hard-earned quality and culturally unpopular today. Paul wrote about the future in 2 Timothy 3:2-5: "People will love only themselves and their money. They will be boastful and proud, scoffing at God, disobedient to their parents, and ungrateful. They will consider nothing sacred. They will be unloving and unforgiving; they will slander others and have no self-control. They will be cruel and hate what is good. They will betray their friends, be reckless, be puffed up with pride, and love pleasure rather than God. They will act religious, but they will reject the power that could make them godly. Stay away from people like that!" What more is there to say?

Jesus, teach me discernment. Give me a clear understanding of righteousness so I can deflect what is unrighteous.

Trust God

A person's steps are directed by the LORD.
How then can anyone understand their own way?
PROVERBS 20:24 NIV

Independence is highly valued in our culture, so it's difficult for believers to understand what a healthy dependence on God looks like. Jesus called himself the vine and his people the branches (John 15:5). We understand that the branches are dependent upon the vine for their lives. When we depend on God, we seek him through the reading of his Word. We'll find wisdom and direction for much of what we need in daily life there.

We also need to seek God through prayer. How do we know if we're praying properly for things that matter? Paul answered that question in his letter to the Roman believers: "In the same way, the Spirit helps us in our weakness. We do not know what we ought to pray for, but the Spirit himself intercedes for us through wordless groans" (8:26). To avoid sinful independence we read and pray. We learn who our King is, and we find out what pleases him.

My Lord and King, may I know you and learn how to please you. May I always prioritize you and your plan for me.

A Wise King

A wise king sorts out the evil people,
and he punishes them as they deserve.
PROVERBS 20:26 NCV

We aren't guaranteed wise leaders in our lives, but we are told what they act like. Today, we read that the bad guys don't get a pass. They are held accountable for their choices, and the rest of us are relieved to hear it. What do we do when our leaders aren't so wise?

There are two things to understand about leadership. First, God puts leadership in place, and we are to respect it for that reason as Paul reminds us in Romans 13:1, "All of you must yield to the government rulers. No one rules unless God has given him the power to rule, and no one rules now without that power from God." Second, God is the ultimate authority: "The Lord has set his throne in heaven, and his kingdom rules over everything," as the psalmist declares in Psalm 103:19. At the end of the day, a human ruler is put in place for now, but whether they are good or evil, God is the ultimate ruler over all eternity and throughout the universe.

Lord, I praise you for your power and dominion. Thank you for your righteousness. I'm grateful for the salvation which will take me to you for eternity.

Steadfast Love

Steadfast love and faithfulness preserve the king,
and by steadfast love his throne is upheld.
PROVERBS 20:28 ESV

Of the thirty-nine books in the Old Testament, over half of them talk about steadfast love. Over a third of the chapters in Psalms discusses it; each of the twenty-six verses in Psalm 136 tells us that God's steadfast love endures forever. Along with God's steadfast love goes his mercy and grace. "The Lord is gracious and merciful, slow to anger and abounding in steadfast love," is found in Psalm 145:8. We are secure in the King because his Word assures us of his enduring love.

This love must be solid and amazing because it preserves the king and upholds his throne in today's verse. It says something about the king's subjects being loyal and true, but it still goes back to the king himself. We have an almighty and worthy king, and his steadfast love gives us endurance and security both now and eternally.

Mighty King, I need you. Forgive my sins and allow me to lean into your steadfast love today. Please give me mercy and grace and show me how to give it to others.

Punishment Rids Evil

Hard punishment will get rid of evil,
and whippings can change an evil heart.
PROVERBS 20:30 NCV

The common definition of corporal punishment is to employ a physical, painful form of punishment as a consequence for actions considered socially or behaviorally unacceptable. Most modern concerns about corporal forms of punishment are in the realm of excessive or abusive uses of it, but many parents support spanking their children with restraint.

God didn't have Solomon write the wisdom of the ages to ask different cultures all over the planet and throughout time if he is worthy to follow. God wrote truth. He is the fount of wisdom, and he knows his creation better than any person. We can trust that an evil heart requires hard punishment to turn that heart around. Truth sets an evil heart free.

Lord, help me place truth front and center in my life. Help me guide others in my life toward you.

A King's Heart

The king's heart is like a stream of water
directed by the LORD;
he guides it wherever he pleases.
PROVERBS 21:1 NLT

The true King follows God. His thoughts and intentions are not random. Almighty God directs and places the purposes of the true King to align with his purposes and plans. The King's inward purposes become God's; his thoughts become God's. He is God. The subjects of the King trust him because they witness the pure results of following him.

Christians follow Christ because he is worthy. We start to see the effects of his Word in our lives, and we give in to him more as we learn how worthy he is; it's more than we could have imagined at the beginning of this walk. We allow him into the depths of our hearts because we trust him more, and we give over the plans for our lives because it is better to follow him than wander after our random thoughts.

Father, keep me close and make me yours. Give me understanding of a deeper relationship with you and help me give you all my trust and faith.

Setting the Standard

Every person's way is right in his own eyes,
But the LORD examines the hearts.
PROVERBS 21:2 NASB

Anyone may appear righteous, and we can fake it for a while, but nobody is fooling God. He knows the intentions of our hearts and sees through every façade. We try to justify our disobedience, but if we're honest with ourselves, we know when we've messed up. Even the evilest people will justify their actions and perceive themselves as doing the right thing; that's why we need to measure everything against God's standard and not human standard.

The prophet Amos said God holds the plumb line. See Amos 7:7-8. A plumb line is a tool that sets the standard for a straight line by which an entire building will be constructed. If we measure each area of a building by a separate standard, it will not align perfectly and will fall apart if it even gets built to begin with. In the same way, God holds the standard for our lives. If we try to follow our personal versions of right and wrong, we will be out of alignment. We will certainly fall apart.

Father God, I can't hide anything from you; you see what lies in my heart. Your standard is perfect, and I choose to align myself with you today.

November

Get wisdom and understanding.
Don't forget or ignore my words.

PROVERBS 4:5 NCV

Diligent Plans

The plans of the diligent lead surely to plenty,
But those of everyone who is hasty, surely to poverty.
PROVERBS 21:5 NKJV

God does not intend for us to live in a *feast or famine* way. Some life seasons are more difficult than others, but he wants us to create healthy habits to live by. He wants us to spend time with him even if we're extremely busy. He wants us to be generous even if money is tight. He wants us to depend on him even if it seems like we have everything under control.

If we don't intentionally spend time with him when our schedules are open, then our time with him will be the first thing we neglect when our calendar is packed full. If we aren't in the habit of living generously when we have extra, then we'll hoard even more when we're barely making ends meet. If we wait until we're in a difficult season to ask him for help, then we're failing to realize we always need his help.

By your strength and for your glory, dear God, I want to learn how to work diligently. I commit to forming and keeping healthy habits. I will not wait until times are tough to turn to you. I need you every day regardless of how the day is going.

Dark Spirits

When you forsake the ways of wisdom,
you will wander into the realm of dark spirits.
PROVERBS 21:16 TPT

Departing from God doesn't happen overnight. Little by little, standards bend, morals loosen, and eyes wander. Our hearts follow our eyes, and our feet turn. Suddenly, we look up and realize we are lost. We didn't *fall from grace* with one big swan dive; we took our eyes off the Lord and took small steps in the wrong direction.

Daily decisions matter. Walking in wisdom means taking intentional, accountable steps and not being led astray by whims and impulses. It may be time to focus on our convictions, community, daily devotionals, and our time spent in prayer. Are we heading in the right direction, or are we slowly stepping off course?

Lord, apart from you, there is no life. Keep me close to you, dear Lord, so I never stray from your side and find myself in the realm of dark spirits.

Pursuit of Righteousness

Whoever pursues righteousness and kindness
will find life, righteousness, and honor.
PROVERBS 21:21 ESV

Why waste our lives pursuing what doesn't last? The pursuit of self-gratification is an empty, worthless existence. This world and its worthless wonders are passing away, but God's kingdom will reign forever. Therefore, let's be devoted to pursuing what will last. We can commit ourselves to righteous living and to being kind. Isn't that more important than getting ahead or being admired?

If our admiration is truly for the Lord, then we won't be so insistent on being admired ourselves. It wouldn't consume our actions and attention. This rat-race way of living leads only to disappointment because Earth doesn't satisfy, and accolades fade quickly. Fame is fleeting and money even more so, but our Father is forever.

Heavenly Father, your Word explains that if I pursue righteousness and kindness, I will find what I am looking for. I will find life, honor, and most importantly you. It is my prayer and pursuit every day to find you.

City of the Mighty

One who is wise can go up against the city of the mighty and pull down the stronghold in which they trust.
PROVERBS 21:22 NIV

A city is organized and implemented through policies and politics. Wherever there are people, there is a need for structure. These structures are held in place through agreements, force, or a combination of the two. Cities also need protection; in biblical times, cities often used thick walls. These strongholds could be overcome but not easily.

Wisdom is more powerful than policies or politics. The opinion of the masses can be swayed, but God's wisdom stands true forever so individual hearts come to know God's wisdom. Policies and politics, both good and dangerous, will come and go; the kingdom of God has perfect policies and politics because they have been implemented by the Almighty God. We can breathe in relief and lean fully on him.

Lord, show me wisdom in the policies and politics around me. Help me know you better so I have the gift of discernment. Help me follow the governments of my land because authority is put in place by you for your purposes.

Tame Your Tongue

One who guards his mouth and his tongue,
Guards his soul from troubles.
PROVERBS 21:23 NASB

Words are like fire: they spread fast and quickly become uncontrollable. Once a word has left your lips, you no longer control it; it has been set free. Think about what words you want running free in the world because many words come back to haunt us.

The Bible warns us about the power of our tongues in James 3:5-6, "See how great a forest is set aflame by such a small fire! And the tongue is a fire, the very world of unrighteousness; the tongue is set among our body's parts as that which defiles the whole body and sets on fire the course of our life and is set on fire by hell." Like fire, our words can offer others warmth, light, and encouragement, or they may cause great harm and destruction. Choose wisely because you can't reclaim a word once it has been spoken.

Your Spirit, dear Lord, offers wisdom and discretion. Teach me to listen and think before I speak. Make me aware of my words and considerate of others.

Bragger and Mocker

People who act with stubborn pride
are called "proud," "bragger," and "mocker."
PROVERBS 21:24 NCV

When we are focused on our thoughts and opinions, we stand on dangerous ground. There is little or nothing stable when we spiral in on our personal thoughts. We can't grow or change if we think we hold intelligence and wisdom within ourselves. Once we let an opinion become truly entrenched, we enter stubborn pride.

God has strong opinions about this behavior. He doesn't think well of pridefulness. It tends to be held by people who have little to back it up. Once the mouth is engaged with stubborn pride, then comes baseless bragging. Once selfishness takes full root, the heart starts to ridicule and mock others. The door opens with pride, and it's a good place to start the walk of humility and grace with the Lord.

Jesus, keep me away from pride. Keep me humble and aware with your Holy Spirit fully entrenched in my heart so there's no room for stubbornness and pride to get a foothold.

Final Victory

The horse is made ready for the day of battle,
but victory rests with the Lord.
Proverbs 21:31 NIV

We can read, pray, and work hard at staying close to God. We can volunteer and work for the kingdom, and that is all good. We can donate and fundraise to ensure the Lord's plans move forward and there will be fruit for the kingdom, but the end of the day belongs to the King.

We don't know the results of each battle, but we do know the war has already been won. We can be hurt or disappointed if God doesn't deliver us a win for our particular fight, but that is where faith is truly tested. The battle may go one way or the other, but it is all in the Lord's plan for the end of the war. God has won; Satan has lost. We will be overcomers with eternal lives in our future. It's all part of the plan.

Keep my eyes on the prize, Father. Whether each of my battles are won or lost, help me trust in you for the final victory.

Better than Gold

Choose a good reputation over great riches;
being held in high esteem is better than silver or gold.
PROVERBS 22:1 NLT

If given the option of riches or reputation, hopefully we would see the worth of a godly reputation. People will do sleezy things for money; it seems almost everyone has a price on their convictions. We need to be a people so sold out we can't be bought for all the wealth in the world. We need to understand intimately the price Jesus paid for us, so no treasure is tempting enough to compromise the truth we hold dear.

We have been bought and paid for, so tell the devil to take his business elsewhere. Walk the road less traveled by choosing full reliance on the Lord. You will be amazed at what he can do through someone who has placed their life and reputation fully into his hands.

Lord, may my reputation always glorify you. I want people to associate who I am with who my King is. A good reputation has far greater value than material wealth, and I deeply desire my life to be an example of someone transformed by the good and gracious God.

Reward for Humility

*The reward for humility and fear of the LORD
is riches and honor and life.*

PROVERBS 22:4 ESV

Pride will end up costing us everything whereas humility leads to a rich and honorable life. When we become tempted to put ourselves first, take our lives in our hands, and deny our reliance on God, let's remember this verse and understand the direction we are choosing.

The only path to life is through God, and fear of him convicts us to make healthy, wise decisions. We haven't yet seen the full majesty of our God, but if we understood exactly who we serve, we would be filled with reverence and holy fear. Yes, he is a loving father who cares for us enough to die. He is also the King and Creator of the universe who will not stand unrighteousness or insubordination. He is love and justice, mercy, and truth. There are consequences for the proud and rewards for the humble.

Lord God, even though humility doesn't come easily, it's imperative to the Christian life. You also reward humility with riches, honor, and life. It's more than I deserve. Why would I be tempted by anything this world has to offer? You are my desire.

Owed a Debt

The rich rules over the poor,
and the borrower is the slave of the lender.
PROVERBS 22:7 ESV

Paul wasted no time telling Christians what they should do about debt in Romans 13:8: "Owe no one anything, except to love each other, for the one who loves another has fulfilled the law." Our money should be secondary to loving one another. Paul also pointed out that being in debt could potentially work against the freedom to love one another.

Money is a powerful force and always has been, but God is more powerful. We are to submit ourselves to God and to serve him first. If we owe anyone money, that needs to be addressed earlier rather than later. It's not a question of where the heart lies; the Lord is telling us we belong to the one to whom we owe money, and he doesn't want his people compromised in that way. Make debt go away, and trust God to help you do it.

Lord, I need you to purge my debt. Help me take each step to do this. Give me persistence and integrity to address this until it is out of my life.

Rod of Discipline

Folly is bound up in the heart of a child,
but the rod of discipline will drive it far away.
PROVERBS 22:15 NIV

Understanding the sinful nature of humanity is helpful when working with children. The Lord brings us children as a blessing as the psalmist states in Psalm 127:3: "Children are a heritage from the Lord, offspring a reward from him." But it's important not to trivialize the fact that children are born into a sinful nature which Paul speaks about in Romans 3:23, "for all have sinned and fall short of the glory of God."

We have been told to teach and train the children over whom we have authority. We have been instructed in Psalm 34:11 about how to do it and what that training should be about. "Come, my children, listen to me; I will teach you the fear of the Lord." To save children from becoming fully entrenched in their own sins, teaching them consistently about God as they grow and learn is an honorable and valuable effort for the kingdom.

Lead me in your way, Lord, when I teach the children whom you have blessed me with. Help me be your voice in their lives so they can know and love you as I do.

Don't Crush

Do not rob the poor, because he is poor,
or crush the afflicted at the gate,
for the LORD *will plead their cause*
and rob of life those who rob them.
PROVERBS 22:22-23 ESV

Our Lord is Lord of the underdog. He loves the oppressed, young, old, poor, and alien among us. He loves the blind, the deaf, the lame, and the mentally challenged. To make this eminently clear, God sent his one and only Son to be born in poverty. He was a baby in a poor family in an oppressed people. Trouble lays heavily on all these people, and God invited trouble to rest on Jesus' shoulders for the ultimate plan of salvation.

1 Samuel 2:8 says, "He raises up the poor from the dust; he lifts the needy from the ash heap to make them sit with princes and inherit a seat of honor. For the pillars of the earth are the Lord's, and on them he has set the world." Things will change; oppression will not last. The poor are challenged now, but they will live in abundance later. Don't neglect any of these people for they hold our Lord's heart. They are his beloved.

Let me see your heart, Lord, and let me see those you love.

Not Like Them

Don't make friends with quick-tempered people
or spend time with those who have bad tempers.
If you do, you will be like them.
Then you will be in real danger.
PROVERBS 22:24-25 NCV

We make choices all day long throughout our lives but deciding to follow today's verse has immediate relief and blessing. We are not to respond in kind to temperamental people. We need to keep God's peace in our hearts and allow it to guide our mouths. We need to avoid those who use volatile speech to stir up emotions because that is not of the Lord, and it has bad repercussions on people around such behavior. Reaching out and speaking about the gospel is primary in importance, but there is a time when avoidance is the best path.

Romans 16:17-18 speaks about such a time. "Look out for those who cause people to be against each other and who upset other people's faith. They are against the true teaching you learned, so stay away from them."

Speak to me, Lord, when I need to leave a situation. Let me know if I need to be the one to step away.

No Lender

Don't agree to guarantee another person's debt
or put up security for someone else.
PROVERBS 22:26 NLT

The poor widow in Mark 12:42 was still paying her way. She didn't have anything left, but she gave her last two copper coins anyway. That is not the situation in our verse today. God tells us to bless the poor in some verses in Scripture but to not assume someone else's debt in other places. It is important we give freely. The first church shared everything they had with each other, so no one was without the essentials. Acts 4:32 says "All the believers were united in heart and mind. And they felt that what they owned was not their own, so they shared everything they had."

To assume someone's debt is a specific and unsavory situation. Christ assumed the debts for each one of his believers, and his ultimate sacrifice set us free. We are to live in freedom, and avoiding debt is part of the plan. Assuming a debt for someone else might seem like a kind thing to do, but it is counterintuitive to how the Lord wants us to live.

Bless me, Father. Let me take to heart every nugget of wisdom you share in the Scriptures.

As He Thinks

For as he thinks within himself, so is he.
PROVERBS 23:7 TPT

Our thought life is the hardest battle to win. Our minds can lead us to wonderful and terrible places. What we spend our time thinking about is a true gauge of where our loyalty lies and what we deem most important. What consumes your mind? Is it God? Your family? Your job? Your future? Movies you've watched, conversations you've had. Are your thoughts negative or positive? Full of hope or worry?

2 Corinthians 10:5 tells us to take our thoughts captive because it isn't wise to allow our minds to wander in a world full of treacherous distractions. The devil will use every ploy to take our thoughts away from God. Consider how many forms of entertainment are constantly before your eyes. It is impossible to go anywhere without advertisements and worldly wonders throwing themselves before us. It requires intentionality, devotion, prayer, and godly contentment to keep our minds fixed on what matters.

Lord, if my thoughts reflect who I am and what I esteem most highly, then please examine my mind, forgive the evil you find there, and call forth anything praiseworthy.

The Future

There is a future,
And your hope will not be cut off.
PROVERBS 23:18 NASB

If you are exhausted or discouraged, remember the future God promised his faithful children. Perhaps life has beaten you down, and regardless of how hard you fight, it doesn't feel like you're winning. Beloved, you have already won! Turn your eyes back to Christ and trust him with your future. Yes, we still need to work hard and be responsible, but we do not need to worry about the future.

Make plans and be wise, but don't lose hope. There is a big difference between diligence and desperation: one works hard but with a heart of peace and faith while the other works fearfully, having given way to hopelessness. If you don't have hope for the future, perhaps it's time to ask God for renewed vision and a reminder that he is faithful and trustworthy. The Lord always fulfills his promises.

Oh God, no matter how bad things become, there is always the promise of a great future with you. I refuse to become discouraged, I cling to your hope, and I choose to follow you. Help me focus on you.

The Wise Son

The father of a righteous child has great joy;
a man who fathers a wise son rejoices in him.
PROVERBS 23:24 NIV

What a relief for parents when their children grow up to be wise adults. It's balm for the soul when children choose the good path. 1 Samuel 13:14 tells us that King David was a *man after God's own heart*. He had many children from many wives, but not all his children loved the Lord like he did. Amnon raped Tamar, Absalom murdered Amnon and later tried to take the kingdom from David, as did Adonijah. On the other hand, Solomon and Nathan are both in the lineage of Jesus Christ. David's children brought him both grief and joy despite his holding God's heart.

Our Heavenly Father experiences all the same emotions over us. Some days we make him proud; other days we hurt his heart, yet his love for us is unchanging. Let's strive to bring joy to our Father in heaven and give him reason to rejoice over us.

Father, I want to be a reason for you to rejoice. I want to walk in righteousness and make you proud.

Reason to Be Glad

Make your father and mother happy;
give your mother a reason to be glad.
PROVERBS 23:25 NCV

In this proverb, there aren't any qualifiers about whether your parents are Christians or even good people. We are told to work to make our parents happy. We invest in them so they will know the love of Christ because they are the parents of one of God's children. If they are also God's children, that's a blessing. If not, the blessing might still be coming because of God's work through us.

Sometimes we need to act in faith. We can make the effort to do the right thing without any knowledge of whether it will make an impact for God. However, we might neglect to remember that every effort for God has an impact on us even if we don't see anything happening outside ourselves. We are changing and growing, and it will have an impact even if we don't see it ourselves.

Lord, keep me persistent in behaving in the way that honors you. Give me tenacity for the kingdom with my parents and my whole family. May my effort bring honor to you.

Give Your Heart

My son, give me your heart,
and let your eyes observe my ways.
PROVERBS 23:26 CSB

When we give God our hearts, we commit to trusting him and following his ways above our own. We admit he knows what is best, and we refuse to worry about anything he said he would take care of. We look to his example and model our lives after him. We love his Word and look forward to spending time with him in prayer and worship.

If spending time with God feels like a chore, you may not truly understand who he is or what he's like. If God's ways seem rigid or unnecessarily restrictive, then you probably haven't yet recognized all the blessings God wants to give you and amazing adventures he wants to take you on.

Almighty God, I am prone to worry and self-reliance. Teach me again and again about your power and faithfulness. Open my eyes to your ways and enthrall me with the great adventure of life with you. Thank you for being patient with me.

Adder Sting

Do not look at wine when it is red,
when it sparkles in the cup
and goes down smoothly.
In the end it bites like a serpent
and stings like an adder.
PROVERBS 23:31-32 ESV

Wine in the cup has a similar beauty to polished gems and beautiful jewels in this passage, but we are told to not be taken in by this beauty. Verse 32 warns that the abuse of alcohol *bites like a serpent and stings like an adder*. The serpent first appears in Genesis to tempt Eve and Adam, and we know how that went. It's best to not trust anything coupled with the bite of a serpent in Scripture.

The adder is a secretive snake that hides rather than confronts. The bite is usually not dangerous except with the weak, and recovery is possible with medicine. Alcohol addiction can be dangerous, but recovery is possible with help.

Lord, open my eyes to any addiction in my life, whether it is wine and spirits or another danger to my spiritual and physical life. Teach me discernment and discretion.

Future Wisdom

Know that wisdom is such to your soul;
if you find it, there will be a future,
and your hope will not be cut off.
PROVERBS 24:14 ESV

God has given us his Spirit to help us navigate this world. Our enemy wants to cut us off from God's grace and steal away our hope and joy. He wants us to fail and fall.

That is why wisdom is so valuable; it recognizes and relies on the promises of God. It can identify and disable the traps of the enemy, and it offers focus and purpose to our lives. A wise person is filled with hope and understanding. They know the devil's threats are easily thwarted when God is on our side. Whatever else you do, first find wisdom.

Thank you, Lord, for giving me your Spirit and wisdom. By your greatness, I can succeed in every good work and escape the snares of the enemy. My hope is in you, and nothing can overcome it.

Get Back Up

The godly may trip seven times, but they will get up again.
But one disaster is enough to overthrow the wicked.
PROVERBS 24:16 NLT

Have you ever been struck down and struggled to get back up? Sometimes one good life-beating is all it takes to knock someone down for good, but not God's children. Remember, we are righteous because of him, so we rise because of him too. We cling to his hope and promises rather than our feeble strength.

Sheer determination can only carry someone so far; eventually we are each met with terrible blows. God promises to always be with us and provide a way through. Unlike others who only rely on themselves, we will never be overcome. We may trip and fall from time to time, but we get up again because our strength comes from God.

Oh Lord, please help me get back up again today. I refuse to stay down and dwell in defeat, but I need your strength to keep going. Give me a kingdom mindset.

Compassion for Enemies

Do not rejoice when your enemy falls,
And do not let your heart be glad when he stumbles.
PROVERBS 24:17 NKJV

Jesus told his disciples in John 13:35, "By this all will know that you are My disciples, if you have love for one another." Love is our brand in a way; it is our undeniable characteristic. We love others not because they deserve to be loved but because Christ has filled us with his love. Therefore, our love is not conditional to the recipient but to the source: God himself.

True Christians love their enemies because we realize they too are made in the image of God and deeply loved by him. We are not to gloat or rejoice when evil people meet destruction. Instead, we ought to pray for their hearts to change. It can be tempting to want revenge on those who have dealt unfairly with us or celebrate when they are met with similar injustices, but God tells us revenge is only for him to enact in Deuteronomy 32:35. It would be wise of us to stick with our calling and leave the vengeance to God.

Loving Lord, fill me with forgiveness and compassion for those who have done me wrong. Thank you for your incredible love.

Convict the Guilty

It will go well for those who convict the guilty;
rich blessings will be showered on them.
PROVERBS 24:25 NLT

Someone who sins against God is always guilty unless they have repented and been forgiven. Whenever someone sins against believers, the sin is still against God. We are completely his, so people who hurt us level their sins against the Almighty. It's not a good place to be.

When a person reaches the point in their guilt when they are worthy of conviction, that sin is serious. This isn't a trite offense but something that requires discipline. Those who hold the guilty one accountable for serious sin will be rewarded and protected. God assures us we will be all right at the end of the day, and we will be rewarded for our efforts.

Thank you, Father, for your righteousness. I am grateful I can depend on you for the line between guilty and redeemed. Keep me humble and make me worthy through the blood of your Son.

Kiss the Lips

Whoever gives an honest answer
kisses the lips.
PROVERBS 24:26 ESV

This proverb is a figure of speech. The kiss in ancient Hebrew connotes affectionate friendship and sincerity. Paul repeats the proverb with his own spin by adding love when he says in Ephesians 4:15-16, "Rather, speaking the truth in love, we are to grow up in every way into him who is the head, into Christ, from whom the whole body, joined and held together by every joint with which it is equipped, when each part is working properly, makes the body grow so that it builds itself up in love."

Emulating Jesus requires this level of integrity and intimacy. We have nothing to hide and only love to show. It is possible to be honest yet not loving, so in a way, Paul advances the ancient proverb with more for believers to understand. We need to emulate Jesus. We need pure hearts to be more like him.

Dear Jesus, teach me more about love. Show me how I can better emulate you to my family, friends, and others in my reach.

Order of Operations

Put your outdoor work in order
and get your fields ready;
after that, build your house.
PROVERBS 24:27 NIV

Getting our ducks in a row can be a challenge depending on the circumstances and our skills. Planning is easier for some people but a horrendous chore for others. No matter our abilities, God wants us to make sure plans are in place and we know the order in which things need to be done.

For believers, it's even more critical to go to the Lord with our plans first as Psalm 127:1 says, "Unless the Lord builds the house, the builders labor in vain." Jesus reiterated the importance of having a plan and carefully seeing it through when he spoke to the crowd traveling with him and recorded in Luke 14:28: "Suppose one of you wants to build a tower. Won't you first sit down and estimate the cost to see if you have enough money to complete it?" Followers of God, whether wired for it or not, will be equipped to do the work the Lord has planned for them.

Teach me, God, for the work you have planned for me. Help me learn the skills I will need to succeed on the path of my life.

Getting Even

Don't testify against your neighbors without cause;
don't lie about them.
And don't say, "Now I can pay them back
for what they've done to me!
I'll get even with them!"
PROVERBS 24:28-29 NLT

Harboring bad feelings or holding a grudge never ends well. Those who love God are told throughout the Word to let God take care of the people who harm them. As citizens of the kingdom of God, we are to behave in love and grace toward everyone, and the Lord sorts out the negative. Paul told the Romans, who were going through horrible persecution in Romans 12:19, "Never take revenge. Leave that to the righteous anger of God. For the Scriptures say, 'I will take revenge; I will pay them back,' says the Lord." If they could follow this advice, we can give it a try.

Even worse, however, is if we're dreaming up crimes committed by people we don't like. If we get as far as lying to condemn them, we've gone over the line. God will correct that behavior.

Father, keep me accountable for what I say. Let me know if I'm out of line and please lead me gently in your way.

The Sluggard

I passed by the field of a sluggard,
by the vineyard of a man lacking sense,
and behold, it was all overgrown with thorns;
the ground was covered with nettles,
and its stone wall was broken down.
Proverbs 24:30-31 ESV

This isn't necessarily a guilt trip for about the state of our yards, but maybe it is. God's people are not to be lazy. There are plenty of things to do as we serve the Lord throughout our lives; laying around indulgently will keep us away from his work.

Work heals a lot of ailments. Research shows that people struggling with mental health issues often need stabilizing schedules, increased competency, and interactions with work to move through difficulties. We don't need to be in a frenzy with all the tasks at home, work, and church, but we need to stay focused and diligent as the Lord places work in front of us.

Lord, keep me in work that honors you and motivates me. Thank you for the work you have brought to me and thank you for your provision. I know both are a blessing.

He Has Answers

It is the glory of God to conceal a matter,
But the glory of kings is to search out a matter.
PROVERBS 25:2 NKJV

We search for God when we need answers, help, hope, reassurance, or anything life-giving. God does not need to search for answers because he is omniscient. He loves to reveal his mysteries to us, but he doesn't just throw them out there; he wants us to search them out. He wants to be pursued. He wants us to realize how desperately we need him, so we seek him.

He's always with us, but do we acknowledge that? Do we turn to him for answers before turning to our friends? God does not need us, but we need him. We need to seek him and not the other way around. If we have questions, he has answers. If we feel hopeless, he gives hope. If we feel unloved or unaccepted, he offers love and acceptance to his family. Search for him.

Father God, you are the King of kings. I trust you with what I don't know because you reveal everything in its time for your glory. Teach me reliance on you alone. Give me persistence to search for you.

Walk with the Wise

A wise warning to someone who will listen
is as valuable as gold earrings or fine gold jewelry.
PROVERBS 25:12 NCV

Find friends who will call you out and warn you if you get distracted by things that don't matter. Surround yourself with people who will help you prioritize properly and challenge you to mature your faith. We need godly examples to point us back to Christ when we begin to wander. Accepting correction is difficult and so is offering it. We need to be willing to accept and offer correction, and we need to walk with people willing to do the same.

We are not expected to avoid messy situations. Jesus got his hands dirty all the time and embraced the mess around him. He loved the unlovable and sought out sinners. He helped them turn their lives around. Let's not ignore the mess or pretend it doesn't exist. We can call it out, work through it, and rise above it together.

I love to listen to you, Lord. Teach me to listen better. Please surround me with wise friends who will encourage me to draw closer to you and prioritize my relationship with you.

December

My child, do not forget my teaching,
but keep my commands in mind.

PROVERBS 3:1 NCV

A Right Word

Use patience and kindness when you want to persuade leaders
and watch them change their minds right in front of you.
For your gentle wisdom will quell the strongest resistance.

PROVERBS 25:15 TPT

Repeatedly we learn that words have power. They can bring positive, godly change if we speak wisely with patience and kindness. Gentle wisdom is sometimes all it takes to disarm the most determined adversary. What is the point in winning an argument if nothing changes? Consider how Joseph, Esther, and Daniel approached their leaders and humbly addressed issues in Genesis 41:14-16, Esther 7:1-7, and Daniel 1:8-14. Their intentions were not to prove they were right but to change the situation.

When we are confronted with resistance, let's remember to approach the issue with patience and kindness. We can put our pride to the side and ask God to use us to bring change for his glory.

Instead of becoming discouraged when an authority makes a poor decision, help me see it as an opportunity to share your truth, dear God. Lead me in wisdom so my words and actions reflect you. I want to have a godly impact on those around me including my leaders.

Giving Way

Like a muddied spring or a polluted fountain
is a righteous man who gives way before the wicked.
PROVERBS 25:26 ESV

Many of us know believers who fell away from their faith. It's tragic and heartbreaking. What was once a beautiful spring or refreshing fountain is now muddied and polluted. The alarming point in today's verse is we're talking about a righteous man. This was someone who feared the Lord yet allowed wickedness to get a foothold in his life.

We can't waver for a moment or think we can handle things alone before wandering around lost and vulnerable for Satan's next ploy. See the warning in 1 Peter 5:8: "Be sober-minded; be watchful. Your adversary the devil prowls around like a roaring lion, seeking someone to devour." We are not victims when this happens; we're choosing to not focus on God and his plans. Be steadfast. Read the Word. Pray without ceasing.

Father, I need you. I need your thoughts so I can know your plans. I need your presence so I can discern truth from lies. Refresh your living water in me.

Honey and Honors

It's not good to eat too much honey,
and it's not good to seek honors for yourself.
PROVERBS 25:27 NLT

Too much sweet food can make a person feel sick; listening to someone constantly praise themselves is just as nauseating. People form their own conclusions about others, and that opinion is based on the character behind the words and not just the words. Someone who feels the need to talk about their own achievements is suspect already. Why are they insecure? What are they hiding? Is there a similar number of bad choices in their background?

We are instructed throughout Proverbs to be conscious of every word we speak. Paul was diligent about teaching humility. He was clear when wrote to the church at Philippi: "Don't be selfish; don't try to impress others. Be humble, thinking of others as better than yourselves" (2:3). Building others up instead of ourselves keeps our hearts in the right place.

Lord, make me conscious of the best parts of people. Show me how to encourage them by highlighting those beautiful things.

Walls of Protection

A man without self-control
is like a city broken into and left without walls.
PROVERBS 25:28 ESV

Is it hard to control your temper? Do people get under your skin easily? A city without strong walls can easily be broken into and overcome, but a well-built city can withstand attack. Similarly, if our self-worth is built on something temporal or worldly, it is on shaky ground. If we are prone to anger and don't have control of our emotions, we leave ourselves vulnerable to attack.

However, if our identity is rooted in Christ and our self-worth comes from what he says about us, we are well protected. The enemy's attacks and lies are not going to pull us away from the truth we know. A person with self-control will not be overcome by the onslaught of the enemy because they hold higher ground.

Lord God, please protect and guard me from my enemy. Help me control my emotions, especially my anger. I don't want to give the devil an entry point into my heart; only you are welcome there.

Don't Roll Uphill

Whoever digs a pit will fall into it;
if someone rolls a stone, it will roll back on them.
PROVERBS 26:27 NIV

Work is a good thing unless it's for naught. If work is done for wrong reasons or selfish intentions, it will not point others toward heaven, and it will not edify God or us. There's no small amount of work involved in digging a pit or pushing a stone uphill. The amount of hard work is not the point of this proverb.

Both the situations in today's verse address a lack of diligence. Labor is fruitless if it is performed with poor work standards or followed by carelessness. Solomon knew the words of his father who wrote Psalm 7:15-16: "Whoever digs a hole and scoops it out falls into the pit they have made. The trouble they cause recoils on them; their violence comes down on their own heads." Sloppy work or carelessness is not given much grace throughout Proverbs. It's a good message to heed.

Father, open my eyes; keep me alert. Stir my soul to acknowledge pitfalls and potentials.

Flattering Mouth

A lying tongue hates its victims,
and a flattering mouth works ruin.
PROVERBS 26:28 ESV

When we believe in Jesus Christ and love him above all others, is there any place for lies or empty flattery? These are not the characteristics of a child of God. Instead, we confess our sins like 1 John 1:19 says to do and follow Paul's direction in 1 Thessalonians 5:22 to abstain from all evil including lying and flattering. Finally, we start to exhibit the fruit of the Spirit.

Paul wrote to the Galatians about what a true believer looks like in terms of character: "But the fruit of the Spirit is love, joy, peace, patience, kindness, goodness, faithfulness" (5:22). Nowhere in that list is lying and flattering. The beautiful fruit of the Spirit will build people, encourage them, and point to the kingdom. It does not hate or ruin others.

Father, I love you and your ways. May my character show the wonderful characteristics listed by Paul. May I speak love and encourage with kindness.

Busy Praising God

Let another man praise you, and not your own mouth;
A stranger, and not your own lips.
PROVERBS 27:2 NKJV

As Christians, we know the beginning and end purpose for everything is God and his glory. Our self-praise is futile and will fade quickly. Engaging in the praise of our heavenly Father, however, is an eternal engagement. Don't become derailed chasing attention and praise for ourselves. It may feel good for a moment, but ultimately it leads to nothing. Furthermore, it's uncomely to draw attention to our good works. If we're living godly lives, others will notice naturally, and they can draw attention to our good deeds as a testimony of Christ working in us.

1 Peter 5:6-7 says, "Therefore humble yourselves under the mighty hand of God, that He may exalt you in due time, casting all your care upon Him, for He cares for you." God knows we desire recognition, praise, and honor, but he will bring it in his way at his time. It should not come from our lips.

God, I want my lips to be too busy praising you to get caught up in trying to praise myself. May others feel closer and more in love with you because of the words I speak.

Jealousy

Wrath is fierce and anger is a flood,
But who can stand before jealousy?
PROVERBS 27:4 NASB

Human jealousy is an ugly quality; it reeks of possessiveness and distrust. God's jealousy, however, is not only merited, but it also saves us from hell and draws us to him. When we are jealous, it is because someone has what we want. Perhaps we feel threatened, slighted, or underappreciated. Whatever the cause, our response to jealousy should be to bring it before God and ask him to remind us how blessed we truly are.

On the other hand, God has every right to be jealous of us because he is our Creator, Savior, and sustainer. Not only do we exist because of him and for him, but he paid a high price to redeem us back to himself. He is unwilling to share us with the world because he wants—and deserves—his holy church.

Oh Lord, thank you for your jealousy. Thank you for saving me and never giving up on me. I am wholly yours, and I will not split my allegiance with anyone or anything else.

Greater Good

Better is open rebuke
than hidden love.
Wounds from a friend can be trusted,
but an enemy multiplies kisses.
PROVERBS 27:5-6 NIV

A real friend will offer a rebuke instead of lip-service. A good friend cares more about being honest and helpful than being liked. Flattery feels good, but it accomplishes nothing. Honest criticism can help us mature and learn, especially when given lovingly and carefully. God is a true friend who doesn't hide his love. He openly gives his rebuke because he cares about our growth.

If we want to be more like God, we ought to consider what kind of friend we are. Do we only say nice things and avoid uncomfortable conversations? Or are we ready and willing to challenge our loved ones to confront their sins and address the problems? We need friends like this, and we need to be friends like this. Let's be loving and honest so our friends know we are trustworthy and reliable.

Lord, in your love, you rebuke me and set me straight. It feels unpleasant for a moment, but I know it produces greater good in me and helps me dig sin out of my heart. I love your discipline.

Friend's Counsel

Perfume and incense bring joy to the heart,
and the pleasantness of a friend
springs from their heartfelt advice.
PROVERBS 27:9 NIV

Some people are simply pleasant to be around. When you're with them, you feel peaceful and loved. Their words matter to you because they matter to you. Their opinion carries weight because you know their perspective is mature. True friendship is sweet, pleasant, and fills our hearts with joy. When a beloved friend offers advice, we are more apt to listen because of the relationship we share.

God's rules are much harder to follow if we don't have a loving relationship with him. When we know him, love him, and recognize how much he loves us, his commandments are easier to adhere to because we understand he's given them to us in love. The same is true for parents, teachers, employers, and friends. Rules are easier to follow, and advice is easier to swallow, when we know the person loves us and cares about us. Relationships matter.

Lord, thank you for pleasant and mature friends who love me and look out for me. Please humble me so I can hear and appreciate their advice. I need you and others to speak truth into my life.

Prudence

The wise see danger ahead and avoid it,
but fools keep going and get into trouble.
PROVERBS 27:12 NCV

It requires more than worldly cunning and street smarts to predict danger and avoid it. Only God knows the future and can lead us safely through this word's plethora of potholes. It may sound simple to stay vigilant, but it's difficult because of the onslaught of information and messaging thrown our direction every single day.

We need to tune out the noise, stop jumping at every opportunity, slow our pace, and spend time with God. Only by focusing on him can we refocus our lives, gain perspective, and realize which way we ought to walk. God offers us practical wisdom for everyday scenarios if we take the time to patiently listen, read the Bible, pray, and practice prudence.

Father God, please teach me to be prudent and avoid trouble. Give me wisdom and forethought. I don't want to live as the world lives; I want to walk as you walked.

Relationships Take Work

As iron sharpens iron, so a friend sharpens a friend.
PROVERBS 27:17 NLT

Others of the same mind and spirit can help us mature our faith and walk in truth. It takes work and dedication to sharpen iron, and it takes work and dedication to be a friend. Casual friends or acquaintances can't nonchalantly address our issues or polish out our flaws. To build a relationship where there's enough mutual trust and spiritual camaraderie to work through problems together requires a foundation of love and connection. The work of a relationship must first be embraced before two friends can sharpen each other.

The Lord made us to live in community, have the support and accountability of friends and family, and walk through life with others. We are not supposed to hide away in comfortable mediocrity. God's intention is for us to embrace community, relationships, and all the human variables which accompany being vulnerable with others.

Lord, I am so thankful for other believers who challenge and sharpen me in word and deed. Thank you for putting people in my life who speak truth and encouragement to me and who live by example.

Boldness

The wicked flee when no one pursues,
But the righteous are bold as a lion.
PROVERBS 28:1 NKJV

Can you think of a time when you boldly spoke up or acted out in truth? When you're filled with righteous boldness, you understand the truth you're standing on is stronger than the shaky footing of your enemy. The righteous are bold because they know they are right, that God is with them, and that they can't be overthrown. Their conscience is clean and their message important; nothing can thwart their calling.

God gives great boldness when we ask him for it, but it shouldn't be kept in reserve. We're granted boldness so we can act. The wicked run away because they are unsure of where they stand. They know their cause is not justified, and their conscience bothers them. We do not live like that because we have been redeemed. We, the righteous, walk confidently, live boldly, and sleep soundly.

Oh God, thank you for filling me with boldness to stand for you in a world full of corruption. Thank you for giving me a sure place to stand and forgiving me of all my sins. I want to live for you.

Confessions

Whoever conceals his transgressions will not prosper,
but he who confesses and forsakes them will obtain mercy.
PROVERBS 28:13 ESV

Sin eats away at our hearts until we either find forgiveness or grow calloused. Unresolved sin weighs us down so it's hard to move forward or focus on anything else. It wakes us up at night, distracts us during the day, and adds an unnecessary load to our shoulders. Concealing sin is not worth it! The initial conversations and admissions are difficult, but they are imperative to healing, freedom, and moving forward. We can't control how others will respond to news of our sin, but we know God will grant us mercy and strength to overcome sin and forsake it.

God doesn't want us to wait until we've gotten everything figured out before we come to him. He wants us to come to him for help. He has the strength we lack, the forgiveness we need, and the love we desperately yearn for.

Oh God, you offer freedom and forgiveness if I bring my burdens to you and hand them over. Sin is heavy, and I need your help to get away from it. I confess everything to you today and ask for your help to walk in your freedom.

Blameless

The one whose walk is blameless is kept safe,
but the one whose ways are perverse will fall into the pit.
PROVERBS 28:18 NIV

It's not worth it to play around with sin. The effects of sin are destructive and pervasive, and we can't walk the line between living for God and living for ourselves. Choose which camp you belong to and commit to it. Sin pulls us off course and distracts us from what we are supposed to do. On the other hand, God patiently guides us and brings us back when we get lost or confused.

Walking blameless is the only way to avoid all snares and pitfalls, but everyone messes up from time to time. When that happens, correct your course, and follow the voice of our loving Lord. He is always nearby and ready to help the repentant. We don't walk blameless because we are perfect; we walk blameless because we walk with God who has taken away our sins and helps us every step of the way.

Thank you, God, for ordaining my steps and leading me on your straight and narrow path. Please take my hand and keep me from going the wrong way. I want to always walk with you.

Bring Calm

Fools give full vent to their rage,
but the wise bring calm in the end.
PROVERBS 29:11 NIV

Jesus faced confrontation often, yet his response was always calm, controlled, and truthful. He did not back down from the truth he knew and stood for, but he also never lost control or gave way to an eruption of emotion. He was always right and always justified, but he never used justification as an excuse to create chaos or react with rage. Jesus calmed storms; he didn't create them.

As his followers, we can also bring peace and calm. Being peaceful and controlled does not mean we allow sin to go unchecked or we don't become upset in the face of injustice. What it means is our approach is wise, calculated, and controlled. We think about what to say instead of immediately lashing out. Real change can happen when we submit to God rather than our feelings and act in wisdom instead of anger.

God, you have set a high standard for morality and maturity. You have called me as your ambassador of truth and love. Teach me how to live like you in the face of confrontation and injustice. Help me control my anger and be a voice of peace in a world of chaos.

Discipline Brings Delight

Discipline your child, and it will bring you peace of mind and give you delight.

PROVERBS 29:17 CSB

When we think of parenting, we don't think of rest. Being a parent means losing a lot of sleep. Yet in the long run, when children have matured and grown well, they bring delight, and even rest, to their parents.

When God invited us into his family, he knew the sins and selfishness we were bringing with us. He did not require us to have it all figured out before we approached him; he called us so he could help us get rid of our sin. Like a good father, he lovingly disciplines us, redirects our hearts, and leads us. Although our disobedience causes him sadness, he never gives up. He truly delights in us. The more we mature with his help and by his grace, the more we prove that godly discipline produces rest and delight.

I want to delight your heart, Father God. I want to embrace your discipline because I know it's done in love. Sometimes that's hard, so remind me how important and worthwhile it is. I love you.

Divine Guidance

When people do not accept divine guidance, they run wild.
But whoever obeys the law is joyful.
PROVERBS 29:18 NLT

The essence of running wild is to be undirected and without purpose. Many of us have a wild season in our lives, and most of us who have grown past that season recognize it as one of discontentment and sometimes pain. We were searching for something—a peaceful place or a way to like ourselves—so we lived with frenetic energy. We were running away from something, and sometimes it was ourselves.

Joy is the opposite of that lifestyle. The Word brings joy. We calm our spirits by reading the Word and knowing the laws of God. By following God's path to righteous living and seeking and knowing his presence, we find ourselves less frenzied, less wild, and more loving. We find peace and experience joy. This work of the Holy Spirit within us is both shocking and wonderful.

Be my everything, Father. Be my purpose and my peace.
Be my Christ and my calm. I praise you forever.

A Humble Spirit

Pride will ruin people,
but those who are humble will be honored.
PROVERBS 29:23 NCV

There is a reason the Bible repeatedly reminds us to serve others, consider others, put others first, and so on. When we are too self-focused, pride wells up in our hearts until there's no room for love. There's no awareness of God or others, and there's no humility. Pride pushes everything else out of its way and ruins us from the inside out.

True honor is reserved for those who aren't looking for it. Jesus was direct when he explained in Matthew 16:25, "Those who want to save their lives will give up true life, and those who give up their lives for me will have true life." Only God exalts people and honors them. If we go looking for it for ourselves, we will only find a superficial version and waste our time and efforts. Our job is to humble ourselves and give him all honor and glory.

Lord, I praise your name! Thank you for your love, forgiveness, blessings, and continued grace. Please help me overcome my pride and embrace humility so I can continue to grow closer to you and bring honor to your name.

Fear of the Lord

Fear and intimidation is a trap that holds you back.
But when you place your confidence in the LORD,
you will be seated in the high place.
PROVERBS 29:25 TPT

A free person can live unconcerned about the approval of others. They aren't consumed with worry about other opinions. Instead, they are confident in what God says about them, and that is where their identity is. Fear does not hold them back because they walk in the freedom of Christ. They are not intimidated by anyone or anything because they know the truth in Philippians 2:13: "God will continually revitalize you, implanting within you the passion to do what pleases him."

There is nothing we need to be afraid of or intimidated by when our confidence is in the Lord. God works on our behalf, so what could foil our plans? God loves and defends us, so who could knock us down? We fear God, not man, because we understand God holds all the cards. Don't be fooled by someone who talks big but doesn't have a hand to play.

You hold my heart, allegiance, and reverent fear. Nothing else can stand before you, so why should I be afraid?

Word as Shield

Every word of God proves true:
he is a shield to those who take refuge in him.
PROVERBS 30:5 ESV

Many people try to debunk the Word of God, but the Word stands firm. We can trust God, and we can trust the Bible. Every single word is true, and we can depend on nothing more than our Creator and his spoken Word.

In a world of subjectivism, the objectivism of God is amazing. Nothing depends on us; our opinions are precious, but they don't matter for eternity. Our feelings break God's heart, but they don't turn the tide of time. Our relationships come and go, but the only one that matters forever is the relationship we have with God. God is all that means anything, but because of him, each of us and all those around us are everything.

Lord, help me focus on you and take refuge in your Word. Let me know and understand you so I can tell others sincerely and succinctly why serving you is all that matters.

Mystery of Love

There are three things that amaze me
no, four things that I don't understand:
how an eagle glides through the sky,
how a snake slithers on a rock,
how a ship navigates the ocean,
how a man loves a woman.
PROVERBS 30:18-19 NLT

God has created many marvelous wonders in which we get to participate. Step into nature to be reminded of how creative and intricate God's design is. He fashioned every detail in this world for us to live in and enjoy. Also consider the people God has put in your life. Relationships are a gift from God.

Love is remarkable and unexplainable; it is practically a mystery. Even more mysteriously, all the love in the world we feel for one another is simply a reflection of the love God feels for us. We are mirrors capturing the image of real love. It's truly amazing.

Lord, you have created great and marvelous things that I can't fathom. The way love works is impossible to explain or understand.

Four Things Strut

There are three things that walk with stately stride
no, four that strut about:
the lion, king of animals, who won't turn aside for anything,
the strutting rooster, the male goat,
a king as he leads his army.
PROVERBS 30:29-31 NLT

In ancient times, a king was expected to be as brave as any soldier in his army. He needed to be a leader of leaders. Today's verse tells us four things have majesty. The writer of Proverbs 30 was a man named Agur, and he used the three-four structure here and in other places of this chapter. Three examples were animals: the lion, the rooster, and the male goat. The fourth was a king.

Animals have their stateliness within their natures. They come by it naturally. The king, on the other hand, chooses his nature and demeanor, and the animals are an example for him. The lion backs down for nothing; the rooster presents a strong presence; the male goat is stately and ready to fight any who oppose him. When we choose how to present ourselves, we should consider our position and seek the Word for whatever God has to say about it.

Lord, make me aware of my position in life.

Cover Your Mouth

If you have been foolish, exalting yourself
or if you have been devising evil,
put your hand on your mouth.
PROVERBS 30:32 ESV

It's better to physically restrain ourselves than put words out there to damage ourselves and others. It's better to remove ourselves from a situation before we engage with sinful intent than create the need to go back later with an apology. It's better to take time with God and in the Word than boast about ourselves and suffer retribution later.

God asks you to pause. Think about what you are about to say. Consider the consequences of your words and don't put yourself in a position where you must backpedal and make up for the damage. Consider what it means to be a child of the living God and let whatever comes out of your mouth reflect your redeemed state and not your sinful nature.

Lord, I am unworthy, so I ask for forgiveness now. I constantly say things I wish I hadn't. Please teach me to control my words and only speak things that edify you and bring joy to those around me.

Beat the Cream

As the beating of cream yields butter
and striking the nose causes bleeding,
so stirring up anger causes quarrels.
PROVERBS 30:33 NLT

A beating isn't a bad thing for cream. Butter is lovely, so the cream is wonderful both before and after. Striking the nose is not lovely. Christ didn't raise a finger when he was innocent but beaten. We may not have the strength Jesus had in the face of this persecution, but he tells us to call on him and he will give us everything we need in that moment. Paul wrote about his own weakness in 2 Corinthians 12:9 when he appealed to the Lord: "Each time he said, 'My grace is all you need. My power works best in weakness.' So now I am glad to boast about my weaknesses, so that the power of Christ can work through me."

We don't need to provoke or engage in anything infused with anger. We have the Prince of Peace dwelling in us. We can give him power over our lives so we can respond as he did.

Dear Jesus, give me the power to control my tongue. Give me the ability to see a situation with your eyes so I'm strong enough to lean into you for guidance.

For the Defenseless

"Speak up for those who cannot speak for themselves; defend the rights of all those who have nothing."
PROVERBS 31:8 NCV

Little children, people who can't hear, people who are otherwise disabled, the elderly who can't think as clearly as they once did: we are surrounded by people who need a voice to speak for them. Do not hesitate to defend others' rights. It is a holy and wholesome thing to do for God's people.

Be glad when your eyes are opened to an opportunity to be God's voice. Be honored when you are chosen to speak for others; it means God has seen you are capable for this task. Be ready for the moment when you have grown past correcting your sins and you are privileged to intervene for the victims of someone else's sins.

Keep me on my toes, Father, so I may serve you in defending the defenseless. Let me see where I am useful to your kingdom.

Worth

Who can find a virtuous wife?
For her worth is far above rubies.
PROVERBS 31:10 NKJV

In a world that lives by the clock, chasing the dollar, let's be people who value virtue. Let's prefer morals over money, character over cash, and righteousness over rubies. A virtuous person brings blessings to their family, value to their workplace, and honor to God.

Why are we consumed with worldly riches that will not last? We can instead refine the hidden places in our hearts which will have an eternal impact on our lives and on those we are closest to. As Christians, it's time we got our priorities straight and focused our time and energy on things that matter. What do you look for in a spouse? What do you hope for in your children? What sort of employee do you want working for you? What kind of person do you want to be?

Above all else, God, I want to be like you. I will put my time and efforts into things that matter.

Enrich Life

Her husband can trust her,
and she will greatly enrich his life.
She brings him good, not harm,
all the days of her life.
PROVERBS 31:11-12 NLT

As Christians, we are all members of God's family and work together within the body of Christ. Therefore, we should never try to tear each other down or harm another believer in any way. Doing so brings harm to all of us and cripples the body of believers. Instead, let's learn how to support each other, make amends, be a blessing, find a way to overcome differences, work together, humble ourselves, act in love, and enrich the lives of others.

We are called to be good, trustworthy, helpful people. Our mission ought to be love. Instead of fighting for ourselves, remember it's God who fights for us, and let's fight for each other. Even the most difficult Christian is a brother or a sister, so consider it a God-given challenge to learn how to break through and bring life instead of strife to that person.

Heavenly Father, please use me to enrich the lives of others. I want to be a bearer of blessings and not a burden.

Strength and Honor

Strength and honor are her clothing;
She shall rejoice in time to come.
PROVERBS 31:25 NKJV

Tough times are telling. Anyone can look put together and strong when they are undisturbed. Pull the rug out from under someone, and you can see who they truly are. How do you react when your world gets turned upside down? Who do you run to when you're given bad news? What are your first assumptions when disappointment smacks you in the face?

Life happens to all of us, but it won't be the undoing of a righteous person because they are clothed with God's strength and honor. They know their endgame is God, their purpose is for God, and everything they have comes from God. The rug does not matter because they're already standing on unshakable ground. They rejoice in the truth which grounds them when everyone else is panicking and scrambling. They are certain when others are unsure. They are calm when the world is chaotic because this world doesn't hold their hope. They are the epitome of strength and honor because, no matter what comes their way, they can't be shaken.

Powerful Lord, clothe me with your strength and honor.

Wisdom and Kindness

Her teachings are filled with wisdom and kindness
as loving instruction pours from her lips.
PROVERBS 31:26 TPT

There are moments in life that define us, but those moments didn't make us. The groundwork had already been laid and the decisions already made leading up to that point. We act on what we've already built.

Do we make selfish decisions because, up until that point, we lived for ourselves? Or do we make a selfless decision because we've lived a life of serving God and others? When we speak, what comes out of our mouths? Is it bitterness, complaint, and self-promotion? Or is it wisdom, kindness, and love? Does what we say have a negative or a positive impact on others? Are we striving to bring glory to ourselves or to God? Our words reflect our hearts, and there will be moments when our hearts are exposed by what we say. Let's lay a godly framework right now and create a habit of good decisions. When moments arise, our reactions will be wise and kind.

I am led by your Spirit, oh Lord Almighty. You guide me and teach me when to speak. Because I listen to you, my words are filled with wisdom and kindness that only comes from knowing you.

Fear the Lord

Charm is deceitful and beauty is passing,
But a woman who fears the Lord, she shall be praised.
Proverbs 31:30 NKJV

Fear of the Lord sparks a courage and tenacity brighter than any youthful vigor or charisma. Those who fear the Lord remember his majesty and worthiness. Consider women of the Bible who were praised and well-esteemed: Sarah, Hannah, Jael, Deborah, Ruth, Naomi, Esther, Abigail, and Mary. We don't know what these women looked like, but thousands of years later, we still talk about them and admire them because they feared the Lord and were obedient to him.

Now think about examples of godly men and women today. What sets them apart? What do they focus on? There is no harm in looking nice, but do efforts to appear beautiful or handsome overshadow our efforts to live blameless and praiseworthily? How do you want to be remembered?

God, don't let me forget what is important and lasting. Thank you for the godly examples you have put in my life and recorded in your Scriptures. Please make me a godly example for others as well.